T0381165

'ASSASSIN'

THE
CONWAY WITTEN
STORY

MARK L. BROTHERS

authorHOUSE

AuthorHouse™
1663 Liberty Drive
Bloomington, IN 47403
www.authorhouse.com
Phone: 833-262-8899

Published by AuthorHouse 11/16/2023

ISBN: 979-8-8230-1296-6 (sc)
ISBN: 979-8-8230-1295-9 (e)

Library of Congress Control Number: 2023914959

Print information available on the last page.

Any people depicted in stock imagery provided by Getty Images are models, and such images are being used for illustrative purposes only. Certain stock imagery © Getty Images.

Cover Photo: Conway racing the dragster at National Trails Raceway Park near Columbus, Ohio Auto Imagery Photo

This book is printed on acid-free paper.

CONTENTS

CONTENTS

FROM THE AUTHOR

I've written dozens of newspaper and magazine articles beginning in 1978, and this is my fifth book since 2010; all are nonfiction stories; however, I found myself running the gamut of emotions on this one; cheering, weeping, laughing, excited, and angry with somber and surprising moments. Conway and Carla, the prominent figures in this account, shared a similar experience.

Conway, who has been trying for nearly twenty-five years to get this story written and published, felt the same emotions with each edit during this exhausting trip to the past, reliving the best portions of his life and the worst ones too. He told me several times that he broke down and cried during the writing process, and I heard his anger and laughter.

For Carla, I heard the anxiety in her voice, listened to her weep, and felt her emotions during our talks. This process was challenging for her; I want to thank both people. I want to hug them and see them both smile. They shared their hearts and souls throughout the time it took to tell their stories.

This book is a true story and was partly developed using dozens of pages of written memoirs by Conway Witten. The balance of the information used in this book was obtained through lengthy interviews and research conducted by the author. Some names have been changed to protect that person's privacy.

I want to thank the following people that helped make this book possible: Conway and Carla, Chuck Belanger, Gordon Holloway, Mike Farrell, Bob Toy, Jeff Taylor, Dean Harvey, Mike Pustleny, Tony Clark, Jim DeFrank Sr., Jim DeFrank Jr., Leon Clark, Matthew Oaks, Garry Merrick, Gale Powley, Dr. Raymond Moody, Debbie Jones, Bobby Davis, Gary Crain, Dr. David San Filippo, Jason Lancaster, and Terri Simmons.

I also want to thank my in house editors for their tireless contributions throughout this project, Garna Brothers, and Julie Chew

Mark Brothers
March 2023

CONWAY'S DEDICATIONS AND ACKNOWLEDGMENTS

Dedicated to Bill and Wanda Witten, my friends, and Carlotta Ann Pace

I would like to thank the following people for their help and contributions throughout my life. Conway Witten, March 2023

- ➢ **Bill and Wanda Witten,** for all your love and sacrifice
- ➢ **Tony Clark,** for being a perfectionist
- ➢ **Wimpy Christmas,** for guiding me on my first journey into racing
- ➢ **Chuck Belanger,** you sacrificed everything for me
- ➢ **Gordon Holloway,** my connection to go fast
- ➢ **Mike Keown,** who always made sure I had the best parts.
- ➢ **Mike and C.J. Farrell,** for being the best employers ever
- ➢ **Debbie Jones,** for picking up the pieces
- ➢ **Bob Toy,** my biggest fan and best friend
- ➢ **The Staff** at Competition Automotive Machine
- ➢ **Mark Brothers,** who wrote a story from a bunch of paper in a three-ring binder
- ➢ **God,** for giving me the experience of the afterlife!

CONWAY'S DEDICATIONS AND AFFIRMATIONS

WHY THIS BOOK?

October 3, 2023 will be the 30th anniversary of an event that changed my life forever.

Over the past 30 years, I have been telling this story to friends, relatives, church members, and church committees. It's time to tell the world what God allowed me to see and hear during my near-death experience and, most importantly, what I learned about myself and my faith in God.

Over the past twenty-five years, I have been in contact with several writers that I thought could tell my story in book form, and it never worked out for whatever reason. I tried to put my thoughts down but couldn't organize them well enough. With only one exception, I have no memory of the events that occurred during my accident and at least two months after. With my speech handicap and other shortcomings, I realized I couldn't take on a book project by myself, one that I have desperately tried to get done.

One day in November of 2022, I posted a request on Facebook for a writer to step forward and help me with this project. It was, in my mind, my last attempt to complete my journey. If I didn't get a response, I would cut my losses and move on. To my surprise, a man posted a reply indicating he was a published writer, a car guy, and a Christian. We immediately started corresponding on Messenger, and after a couple of weeks, we agreed to go forward with the book. The man in question is Mark Brothers, originally from southeastern Illinois and now living in Utah. Mark was first published as a freelance writer in 1978 and has since written four books, one about the history of his hometown drag strip. I have great faith in Mark, and we have developed a friendship over these many months.

I was just a middle-class kid growing up in the Midwest with a simple dream; I wanted to be the best at whatever I did. The best at music, playing my instruments in the school band, the best at racing slot cars, the fastest on my sting ray bike, the best model car builder, and the best drag racer. I was surrounded by four first cousins that played professional sports in the NFL and NBA, and the wall of success was set high for me. I wanted to be the best on the job, in racing, and in my relationship with my wife.

I wasn't always successful. Over the years, I failed so many times and made many mistakes, all of which I regret. I also had an inconsistent relationship with our maker, using religion in my selfish ways. I made serious mistakes in my marriage, another case of being selfish. I made mistakes with friends and family that I wish I could change. I want to tell you about the people that made a difference in my life, my family, friends, people on the job, and the people I raced with and against; there are so many. I want to tell you about being bullied, losing everything I ever worked for, and trying to regain it.

Finally, regarding the essential part of this book, after a severe racing accident that nearly took my life, I want to tell you about meeting an angelic being and dwelling in a place where mercy and forgiveness are experienced the entire time you are there. I want to tell you about our conversation, what I saw, what I heard, and what I felt; it was the most incredible experience I have ever had, and it changed my life forever.

Conway Witten
March 2023

FOREWORD

BY BOB TOY

I am happy to present this book about Conway Witten's life story. It has been shared in parts over the years but has yet to be in a complete manuscript. Let me tell you a little bit about our relationship over the years.

I met Conway during the three years I worked in Louisville, KY, in the late 1970s. I was introduced to him by a mutual acquaintance, fellow Kentucky Motorsports Hall of Fame inductee Joe Williamson. It was readily apparent that Conway and I both shared a passion for NHRA class drag racing. My career took me back home to Paducah in 1980, but I kept tabs on his exploits by catching up with him when we crossed paths at racing events. I continued to be impressed by his work ethic and devotion to succeeding at his goals. A big part of Conway's story and further evidence of his work ethic and want-to was that he typically spent 16-hour days, splitting time between Farrell's trucking company and Mike Keown's engine shop in Jeffersonville. His infamous SS/BA 'Hemi Killer' Corvette has to rank high on the list of most impressive NHRA Super Stockers of all time; too bad the executives at Glendora headquarters saw fit to ban it from the competition.

I had begun participating in NHRA divisional and national event competitions in the mid-1980s, so I ran into Conway more frequently at the track. Many sportsman racers, he and I included, wished to participate in the Competition Eliminator category, where there is no 'break out'; in other words, you can't lose by going too fast. Conway marshaled all the resources he could gather and began competing in this division in 1991. Conway hit the ground running, assisted by the resources available at Keown's shop and direction from the ultra-savvy Gordon Holloway of Competition Cams. Succeeding far quicker than the old guys thought he should ("he still needs to pay his dues"), he won the Bowling Green points meet and got to the semi-finals at Indianapolis that year. Even when competing at the same events, I enjoyed hanging around Conway, Chuck Belanger, and Gordon at the track.

Though I had more significant than average success racing in the NHRA Super Stock Categories, my heart wasn't in it anymore. As the end of the 1993 season wound down, I made plans to sell my 1969 Camaro Super Gas car and do something different.

I talked to Conway in the fall and tentatively made plans to attend the Dallas race with him and his crew, which was to be held two weeks after the fateful Topeka event. Though I didn't tell Conway for years afterward, I was planning on approaching him with the idea of joining him and Gordon in their racing endeavors.

I have always been grateful that I wasn't at the Topeka race to witness the horrific crash. I cannot even bear to watch the event on film; as soon as I learned about the disaster, I put into motion plans for establishing the Conway Witten Recovery Fund as a means of helping out with the expenses associated with the wreck. I was overwhelmed by the outpouring of support from the racing community and was glad to do my part in assisting Conway and Carla.

I have kept in touch with Conway since the mishap, and I was honored to give his induction speech to the Kentucky Motorsports Hall of Fame in November 2016. He remains a stellar example of hard work and perseverance in his struggles to continue his walk down the road of life after the life-altering event.

Along the lines of a silver lining to every cloud, my relationship with Conway and work on the recovery fund brought me to know Gordon Holloway much more closely. It took time to determine that he was not through racing at the level of Competition Eliminator, and it gave me the opportunity I had been seeking to get involved there. Our association led to a partnership with Gary and Todd Frantz of Louisville, beginning in late 1994. God blessed us with success at the track beyond my wildest dreams, and the years spent together remain some of my best memories. I hope you enjoy the book as much as I enjoy my friendship with Conway.

Bob Toy
Paducah, KY
March 14, 2023

INTRODUCTION

Topeka, Kansas - October 1993, NHRA Sears Craftsman Nationals

The drag strip, named Heartland Park in those days, was located a few miles from the central portion of the city on the south side. It was only a few years old, built in 1989, and sanctioned by the National Hot Rod Association (NHRA). The quarter-mile track had a great racing surface, and the altitude, only 948 feet above sea level, posed no problem for races in all classes.

In the fall of 1993, drag racer Conway Witten and his crew, comprised of childhood friend Chuck Belanger and friend Gordon Holloway, came to the track from the Louisville, Kentucky, and Memphis, Tennessee, area to compete in the NHRA Competition Eliminator class. Conway had been racing in this class, a very diverse class within the NHRA, since 1991.

Currently, in points earned from racing, he is in third place in his division and fifth place in the national standings. His rear engine dragster was powered by a 340 cubic inch small block Chevy engine hand-built by Conway. He was excited to be at the track for the first time in his twenty-year racing career.

Friday & Saturday, October 1 & 2

While trying to qualify on Friday, the team encountered a few problems. The car wasn't running right, so they changed the rear-end gears, followed by several more adjustments. Still unsatisfied with the car's performance, they called it a day and would wait until Saturday to try again. The next day, although they had already qualified for the competition by the afternoon, they still had performance issues. Conway decided to take the fuel pumps apart and clean them. While in the middle of this task, a spring flew out of the pump and struck him in the eye. He flushed the eye and rested a while, but it was hurting and became light-sensitive. He drove himself to a local hospital while his crew finished his task. He was treated and released, told to take it easy for the rest of the day and that night and to keep the eye dry. They all met back at the hotel room, Conway wanted to clean up and go to bed, and the other two men went out to dinner. Conway called his wife and told her about his day; then, he climbed into the tub.

Taking a bath, he experienced a strange feeling of guilt that gradually overwhelmed him. He was racing at the national level, and although he had a small sponsorship through one of his teammates, it was still costly to race; one run down the track cost more than some people made in a month. This was on Conway's mind, and he began to cry.

Suddenly he felt a presence but saw no one; he heard a voice too and still saw no one. He thought to himself, "I'm losing it." The voice assured him that poor and hungry people would be cared for; it wasn't his fault; wait until tomorrow, and he would learn more. Scared and confused, Conway thought, "If I tell my team what just happened, they are going to think I'm goofy." As he prepared to go to bed, his guilt slowly turned into a serene, peaceful feeling. He fell asleep in that state.

Sunday, October 3

Sunday morning, Conway woke up, and his eye was much better. There was no pain; the sensitivity was gone, so he prepared for race day with his team. On their way to the track, the group stopped at McDonald's for breakfast. He liked to get to the track early on race day, mainly because he was a perfectionist. He went over the car repeatedly, making minor adjustments here and there, checking tire air pressure, fuel source, and looking at the entire car specifically for safety issues.

His dragster could cover a quarter mile in 7 seconds at nearly 200 miles an hour; it had to be safe and reliable run after run. Although he had a team of two other people, he was in control when it came to the mechanics of the car. He did every bit of the wrenching, tune-ups, tear-downs, and rebuilds; he trusted no one else at these tasks. His crew had their duties, loading and unloading the car, ensuring he was at the line when called, spotting him in the burnout box, and guiding him into "the traction zone" on the track as he backed up after the burnout.

His team helped him stage, too, while always looking for oil or fuel leaks. They would drive the tow vehicle bringing him and the dragster back to the pits after every run.

Conway was feeling lucky on this day, and why not? It was his birthday. He was now 38 years old, married to a lovely woman, had a great job, had just built a new home, and was doing something he loved more than anything - drag racing.

He was a successful drag racer who dreamed of becoming a full-time professional. All he needed was one more break, a little boost, and his dream would come true.

Conway wins round after round. His car was running great, he was driving great, and the competition was falling by the wayside. Among his competition thus far that day was David Nickens and Mike Tumble, both world champion drivers. Also John Lingenfelter, a world champion too. He ran the famous Lingenfelter Performance Engineering, specializing in Corvettes and Firebirds, the winner of numerous drag races in this and the pro stock truck class as well. They were all hard to beat, but Conway, the man with no significant sponsorship, building all his engines by hand, had done it.

After winning the semi, Conway made it to the final round. One more win, and he would have another "Wally," some money in his pocket, and additional points. He felt like a winner.

Conway's crew brought him up to the line. He was the first to do a burnout; his competitor, Jeff Krug from the west coast, then did his burnout. Due to a horsepower-to-weight disadvantage, Krug would get a handicapped start.

Both cars were ready and staged, Krug's light turned green, and he launched forward; a fraction of a second later, Conway was off too. His car does a small wheelie on the launch, and the front wheels come up, but the rear wheelie bars stop this motion. Conway's car is 300 feet down the track at over 100 miles an hour in about two seconds when something goes terribly wrong!

The car loses traction, drifts left, and as it gains traction again, the dragster rolls over, while doing a 180-degree turn. The car uprights itself, but when the still spinning rear wheels hit the track surface, the car begins to roll an additional 10 to 15 times while parts of the car fly all over the track. Finally, the car slides to a stop, with the front wheels facing toward the starting line.

The entire event takes only eleven seconds.

When the dragster stopped, announcer Bob Ukifer called for the emergency crews. They immediately respond, and the first care provider to the scene kneels next to Conway, still strapped in the car's cockpit. (In a dragster, the cockpit is open; there is no conventional top on this type of race car) Dan Brickey, the lead NHRA

EMT, a Viet Nam Vet, and former battlefield medic, conducted an immediate medical assessment. "Oh my God," said Dan to his partner, "He's not breathing!"

As of this writing, the crash can be viewed on YouTube at this address <u>https://www.youtube.com/watch?v=fVa-3slItfg&t=15s</u>
Or, search Conway Witten Crash.

CHAPTER I
GROWING UP
1955 to 1973

Shively, Kentucky, October 3, 1955

Wilmoth Conway Witten Junior was born on Monday, October 3, 1955, to Mr. and Mrs. Wilmoth Conway Witten Senior in Shively, Kentucky, a suburb of Louisville. Junior was the first child born to the Witten's, who were married in 1953.

Wilmoth Senior was born in Bonnieville, Kentucky in 1922. His friends and family nicknamed him "Bill," which he used all his life. He joined the Army during World War II serving in the 5th Army under the command of General Mark Clark. Bill's experiences during the war were extensive, seeing action in North Africa, Sicily, and Anzio Beach. He shipped home after his overseas tour and served the rest of his enlistment as a Military Policeman in Virginia. Upon his honorable discharge, Bill had a chest full of decorations and memories, some of them dark, hidden from everyone else for the rest of his life.

"Dad seldom talked about his time overseas," said Conway. "I'm sure he had bad memories of his tours of duty; he was exposed to a lot of killing." Although Bill barely spoke of his time in the Army, he enjoyed watching war movies and the T.V. series "Combat," starring Vic Morrow, the longest-running World War II drama on T.V. that aired during the 1960s for six seasons.

Conway's mother, Wanda Jervis, was born in Corbin, Kentucky, in 1931. She left for Shively right out of high school in 1950 and moved in with a sister who lived in a new housing project built after the war. Wanda found employment at Jones and Dabney, a chemical factory first opening its doors in the mid-1930s. During Wanda's time at the plant, she met Bill, who was in the maintenance department and was responsible for repairing and running all the different systems. They started dating, fell in love, and were married in 1953. She was twenty-two, and he was thirty-one.

1

Bill would remain at the plant for forty years, while Wanda left the company when she became pregnant with her first child.

The Wittens moved into a brand new home shortly after Conway was born, a gift from Bill's father, a home builder and developer in the area. The house was small but brand new and big enough for three. In 1956, shortly after their second child was born, Bill's father presented them with another new home. This one had a full-size basement. "The basement was unfinished, and the home had only two bedrooms and one bathroom. After the third son was born in 1959, all three boys slept in one bedroom until we got into our teens. That's when Dad finished the basement and built two more bedrooms down there," said Conway.

The Witten household was like most middle-class households from the late '50s through the '60s. The boys played little league baseball, and attended summer recreation activities at Rockford Lane Elementary. There were backyard Bar-B-Q's, summer swimming and occasional fishing trips. They went shopping with their mother, and went to the movies. All three boys were close enough in age to grade school together.

Wanda never learned to drive, but it was not for lack of trying. She experienced a near miss while behind the wheel with Bill as the instructor. This convinced her never to try it again.

In the early 1960s, Conway's Uncle Ed was in the Air Force. That's when Conway became a high-performance jet fan, especially the Lockheed F-104, otherwise known as the 'missile with a man.' He started checking out books from the school library on the subject. "I always had an airplane book in my hands back then," he said. "I would memorize the specs of all the planes, the faster and more advanced the better."

Like many of us at a young age, Conway didn't escape the affectionate nickname phase in his life as his mother and other family members called him 'Conny.' "Have a good day at school Conny", his mother called as he walked to the school bus one morning.

When he got home that afternoon, he immediately protested to his mother and begged her to stop calling him that, at least in front of the other kids. The kids had overheard his mom call him 'Conny,' and by the time the bus arrived at school, they were calling him 'Connie Francis,' after a famous female singer of the era.

The next morning in a deliberate attempt to save his pride, Conway's mother walked him to the bus stop and loudly proclaimed, 'Have a good day at school,

CONWAY!" Satisfied with his mother's brave deed, he found a seat and sat down. Several kids called out as the bus took off, "Good Morning, Connie!"

Conway was about ten when his neighbors, Russ and Helen Kramer, set up a slot car track for their kids. It was a massive track, homemade out of wood, with six lanes and a high bank turn that covered the entire basement floor. Conway was invited to come over and watch the racing. He was excited about the setup and wanted a car of his own to race.

Slot - car raceways proliferated in the 1960s. At its peak, the hobby generated half a billion dollars a year in sales, with as many as 3000 racetracks in the United States alone. The tracks were massive in the area and could usually accommodate up to ten cars at a time. The home setups were usually figure-eight tracks for up to two vehicles.

Conway said, "I remember my very first slot car; it was a COX-produced Ford GT, and Russ Kramer built it for me. We would spend hours racing those cars in his basement. We also went to the hobby shop at Dixie Manor to race, sometimes spending the entire day there."

The Kramer's not only loved slot cars, they loved cars period. "They always had a couple of fast drivers parked in their driveway," Conway remembers. "I love muscle cars, and when Russ and Helen bought their new 1969 Mach 1 with a 428 Cobra Jet, I fell in love with it," Their son Jackie got a new one that same year; his was a Super Cobra Jet.

A few years later, Conway bought the Kramer's Mach 1. He modified the engine with a hotter cam, intake/carburetor, and headers.

Conway played sports, too, and in 1966, when he was about eleven years old, he experienced his first sports-related injury. While playing tackle football with many friends, he hurt his right knee. The damage was severe enough for a hospital stay; the affected leg was in traction for several days, then a cast for three weeks.

In the fourth grade, Conway started playing the clarinet, and when he entered the seventh grade, he joined the band. He would be in the marching band and the orchestra for four years, playing the clarinet, oboe, and bassoon. According to Conway, it was just a phase he was going through because he became bored and left the band after his sophomore year in high school.

In 1966 Conway's Uncle Russell took him to see the movie "Grand Prix." That's when he discovered formula one racing (Indy type cars) and became a loyal fan of Jimmy Clark, a famous racer who drove a Lotus Ford. In addition, the Cam-Am road racing series was starting, featuring drivers such as Parnelli Jones, Jerry Titus, Peter

Revson, and Mark Donahue. They drove slightly modified versions of the Z/28 Camaro, Boss 302 Mustang, and the Cougar, some of his favorite cars.

"I remember hearing about Jimmy Clark's accident at the Hokingham facility in Germany," Conway said. "He was killed and I stopped following Formula One racing for twenty years." When driver Aryton Senna began racing in the same series Conway became a fan and followed his career. Sadly, Senna was killed during racing action at San Marino, Italy; a head injury caused by a piece of flying debris that pierced his helmet.

When it came to religion, Bill and Wanda didn't attend church on a regular basis. "It was only on special occasions that we went to church together," Conway remembers. "And that wasn't very often." Conway remembers attending church with the Kramer family and on occasions with his Uncle Russell. "I went to Sunday school and church services with the Kramer family off and on from the time I was in grade school until high school, at the Rockford Lane Baptist Church."

When it came to being the family's breadwinner, Bill was a good worker and even coached his boys in little league baseball, a sport he truly loved. He was a St. Louis Cardinals baseball fan, and during the season, he would sometimes sit in his car listening to the games on the radio.

This wasn't the only reason he chose to be alone. According to Conway, his father was an alcoholic, and bourbon was his choice of drink. Wanda objected to his drinking, even to the point of confrontations, but she never seriously pushed the issue. She loved Bill and put up with his choices.

The entire family knew about the drinking, Bill wasn't fooling anyone. The kids would find empty whiskey bottles hidden under chairs, stuffed in the cushions of the couch, and in other places throughout the house while growing up. Their father wasn't a mean drunk and never laid a hand on his family under the influence or otherwise, so that wasn't a worry. He was a loner when he drank; Wanda and the kids rarely saw him actually drinking, but obviously he was.

It was a different era compared to now. Adult drinking in the '50and '60s was more acceptable. Although on occasion Wanda searched for help regarding the issue, there were limited resources.

There's a verse in the song "Country Boy" by Aaron Lewis where he talks about his grandfather, a WWII Veteran. "My grandfather was a drinker; back in the day, he put 'em down; a war is known to change a man, whiskey is known to change a man." At the time, the Witten family didn't know that their father was more than likely suffering from post-traumatic stress disorder, PTSD, which hundreds of WWII vets suffered from but were never officially diagnosed. The official terminology used back then was "Shell Shock" and "Battle Fatigue," but there were few options for the vets during this time. Many turned to alcohol to help them cope with the issues.

Although researchers and physicians knew that there was a mental disorder among the vets due to their personal wartime experience, especially after WWII, PTSD wasn't officially recognized by any agency as an illness until 1980 when the American Psychiatric Association (APA) added PTSD to the third edition of its Diagnostic and Statistical Manual of Mental Disorders. The Veterans Administration soon followed.

In early 1969 new neighbors moved in just one house down from Conway, their names were Tony and Donna Clark. Tony was 25, and Donna was a couple of years younger. He worked at Union Carbide, and she worked for a local radio station.

The cool thing about this couple was their love for cars and drag racing. Tony drag raced a '56 and '57 Chevy, and his everyday driver was a '66 GTO; it had a 389 with three deuces and a four-speed with a factory-installed reverb for the stereo. His wife drove a '66 Chevelle.

Tony and Donna befriended Conway and invited him over for dinner often. They included him in their softball games, took him to drag races, and Tony let Conway help him while he worked on cars. This was the beginning of Conway's love for drag racing, working on cars, and engine building. A seed was planted, and it began to grow.

That summer, Tony was rebuilding a 390 cubic inch engine from a '67 Fairlane G.T. and invited Conway to help. He explained everything he was doing in simple terms, and Conway was a fast learner. "I didn't know much about the rebuilding process then. I washed parts, helped where I could, and watched and listened to Tony," said Conway.

Tony reminisced, "Conway was only 13 when we first met. I had a '55 Chevy that I drag raced locally." After Tony got to know Conway better he took him to the drag strip for the first time. "I watched the races that day and immediately became a huge fan," said Conway.

"I did all my work at home, just shade tree stuff. I didn't even have a garage," he said. Tony did his engine work in the basement of his home, hauling the block, and other engine parts in and out separately using a two wheel dolly.

"Conway was always at my house back then. I taught him the basics of engine building during a three year period. I'd come home from work, and he would be there waiting for me to teach him something new. He was a fast learner, astute, always asking questions; my goodness, after a couple of years, he started making recommendations to me on how to make the car go faster!"

When Tony introduced Conway to drag racing, he told him about the history of the sport as well. Commercially, drag racing started with the opening of the Santa Anna drag strip at an old airport in Orange County, California. Creighton Hunter and C.J. "Pappy" Hart opened the track in 1950 for "straight line" racing. The distance of the track was one-quarter of a mile, 1,320 feet. This was based on the track length of quarter horse racing. Soon 1/8th of a mile or 660-foot tracks would open too.

Drag racers would stage their cars at the starting line and, once started (flag men were first used to start the races, and later electronic systems using different colored lights were used), would accelerate the entire length of the track, trying to be the first to cross the finish line.

Drag racing grew in popularity to the point of fielding hundreds of full-time professional drivers that traveled the U.S. competing against each other for money, trophies, sponsors, and popularity. U.S. auto manufacturers used the "Win on Sunday, sell on Monday philosophy."

Tony and Conway soon became more than friends because, to Conway, Tony was like a big brother; to Tony, Conway was more of a son. Conway would eat supper with the Clarks two and three times a week, and the entire time it was bench racing, and nothing about cars was out of bounds. Tony and Donna even introduced him to the drive-in restaurant "Dizzy Whiz" in 1970; drive up and a car hop will take your order and deliver your food when ready. Opening in 1947, it is still in business today and one of Conway's favorite places to go.

In October, now fourteen, Conway was officially a "Car Guy Club member." He was car crazy in many ways, still racing slots, building models, reading all the car magazines and slowly getting away from playing sports as he had when he was younger. Not old enough yet to drive, he is yearning for more and more car knowledge and experience. One day that same year his father drove home in a brand new Ford Torino G.T. with a 351 V8 and four barrel carburetor.

"I would go into the garage and set in that car and dream of driving it," Conway explained. "I would pretend I was on a track and racing, taking the curves, racing down the straights; it was so cool to be in that car." To make his adventures a little more realistic, Conway would turn on the radio as he cruised down his pretend highway, and suddenly he discovered the current music scene. "The music in 1969 was the best, CCR, Grassroots, Blood, Sweat and Tears, Steppenwolf. I loved all of it."

During this time, Conway started his first real job delivering the local paper on a route. Every Monday through Saturday, Conway was on his metallic green Schwinn Stingray, providing the daily news. He doesn't remember much about the route now with two exceptions; his route manager had a new Super Sport Chevelle with a 396 V8 and cowl hood, it was red with black stripes, and he met and befriended some new friends.

Conway met Wimpy and Della Christmas, a married couple only five years older than him, and they were into drag racing too. Wimpy worked for an auto parts store and Della was a secretary for a local business in town.

Now, between Wimpy and Tony, Conway had two mentors that he could learn from, picking up more than anyone realized by just listening and watching. Tony already had a clue that Conway had skills, Wimpy would learn this too, but no one knew the actual reason why Conway learned so fast, retaining all that knowledge and eventually becoming a teacher to both men. Conway didn't know either, he just loved to learn. A few years later, the answer came; Conway's IQ level was officially rated extremely high.

As time passed, Conway saved his paper route money and bought a go-cart body later in the year. As a present, his mother got him a West Bend 820 (8.2 cubic inches) engine. Conway installed the engine with help from Tony. The engine, pumping out ten horses, made the little cart super fast, and Conway and Tony started riding it in a local school parking lot after hours. "I couldn't believe how fast that little thing was," says Conway.

"One day Tony was driving it at the parking lot and Donna was there too. We marked out an oval, and Tony was flying lap after lap. I asked Donna, why is Tony smiling so much?" Donna said, "He's not smiling; he's determined to go faster each lap; he's gritting his teeth!" "That's the way Tony was, and that's how I was going to be too!"

1971

If ever there was an important date in his life, this was it: October 3, 1971, Conway celebrated his 16th birthday. He was excited about getting his license, as most young men are. A driver's license meant freedom and independence.

All sixteen-year-olds wanting a license in Kentucky had to attend driver's education. Once this was completed, they had to pass a written and driving skills test. He became a legal, licensed driver on Wednesday, November 3, 1971. Conway's parents had presented him with his first car, a first-generation Mustang, a 1965 hardtop, maroon in color, with a 289 four-barrel and four-speed transmission.

The legendary Ford Mustang was first introduced on April 17, 1964. Debuting at the World's Fair and every Ford Dealership in the United States as a 1964 ½ model, 22,000 were sold on the very first day. In the first 12 months, Ford sold over 418,000 Mustangs consisting of two-door hardtops, two-door fastbacks, and two-door convertibles, breaking all their previous sales records.

December 23, 1971

Seven weeks later, Conway wrecked the car. "I was getting on it, going through the gears, and didn't see a car stopped in front of me until it was too late. I slammed on the brakes, went sideways, and hit a parked car on the passenger side of the Mustang. A stupid thing to do," said Conway. No one was hurt, he had insurance, and after the police cleared the accident scene, he drove the car home with his tail between his legs. Another embarrassing side note is that Conway had an uncle who was a lawyer, and the accident occurred right in front of his law office.

In 1971, Conway was hanging out with Kenny Bowman, his best friend. They would have several adventures with cars and girls over the next year and weren't beyond "pulling the wool' over the eyes of their parents. Conway tells a story about a girl Kenny was seeing who lived in Glasgow, Kentucky, nearly 100 miles from the Louisville area. Kenny's parents did not favor him seeing this girl after finding out where she lived, so they checked the odometer on his car regularly.

One evening the boys just had to visit; the girls wanted to go to a local dance with them. Conway came up with a plan. He crawled under Kenny's car, unhooked the speedometer cable from the transmission, and off they went. This trick would keep the odometer from registering miles, but the driver would no longer be able to monitor his speed. Once the boys drove back to Louisville, Conway would hook the speedometer cable back up. The plan worked until a few later, Conway forgot the cable and Kenny, driving by himself, got pulled over for speeding. The officer approached the car and asked, "Do you know how fast you were going?" Kenny started to tell the whole story to the officer but decided against it. He simply said "No sir, I don't, my speedometer doesn't work."

In 1972 Conway was a junior in high school and started to plan his future. What would you think his choice of occupation would be? Well, it's not what you would expect. He signed up for some advanced classes at school, one was called Comparative Anatomy. That's because Conway was planning to be a doctor; however, that was short lived.

The class met at the University of Louisville hospital, and the very first assignment was to observe an E.R. doctor suture a nasty laceration on a work-related injury a local man had experienced. "As the students asked questions during the procedure, I became sick. With each question, I got sicker and had to leave the room. I didn't realize the site of blood would do that to me," Conway admitted, laughing about it now.

His first prom came that spring, and Conway would take a young lady he had been dating from the local area for a while. She was beautiful with big blue eyes and dark hair and had become a important person in his life. "I invited her to prom but she broke down crying and told me she couldn't afford a dress for the occasion. She came from a low-income family, and I was embarrassed after asking her," he said. At home the next day, Conway told his mother about the problem, and Wanda decided to help. She contacted the young lady and picked her up one afternoon. Wanda took her shopping and bought her a prom dress. Conway and his girlfriend attended the event and had a great time.

In the spring of 1973, Conway's senior year was slowly coming to an end. He was attending school in the mornings and working at Best Photo Industries in the afternoon, a situation brought about by loading up on credits the first three years of the high school allowing him time to get work experience and graduate too. Conway bought his second Mustang, a red '66 convertible, 289 V8 four-barrel with an automatic transmission.

After many weekend nights bench racing at Wimpy and Della's house, and several trips to the drag strip as a spectator and guest of Tony, Conway was ready for the track. He wanted to experience what it was like drag racing on a legal track against the competition. Wimpy agreed to go too and followed him to a drag strip called Cedar Creek, right outside Louisville.

April 21, 1973, Cedar Creek Drag Way, Louisville, Kentucky

Conway's first race on an actual drag strip occurred on Saturday, April 21, 1973. He uncapped the headers on the Mustang, put the convertible top up, rolled up all the windows, and got behind the wheel. "My car wasn't speedy because it had a high gear rear end and wasn't tuned properly that day," Conway said that he felt weird pulling up to the line, a little unsure of himself and the car.

During the first run, his car "leaned out," too much air in the air /fuel mixture of the carburetor caused it to miss and run poorly in high gear. At the time, he didn't know the problem was carburetor related, but back in the pits Wimpy explained what to do. Conway did his best to make adjustments without any fundamental tools or parts. He went for the next run, this time he was up against a '70 Chevelle. The lights turned green and off they went down the strip; the Mustang was running much better and was closing in the Chevy. Just as the two cars crossed the finish line, the Chevelle blew a flywheel, sending debris into the windshield of Conway's car. "I often wonder if this was a sign of things to come," laughed Conway.

It was a close race but Conway won by a bumper. As he drove back to the pits Conway remembered going to see his first drag race with Tony four years earlier, that had hooked him as a fan, but now, he knew driving was even better.

CHAPTER 2
RACING AND WORKING, THE EARLY DAYS
1973 – 1979

Conway graduated from high school in June 1973. He was 17 years old and didn't drink, smoke, or do drugs. A rare situation for that time period, but his father's drinking had soured Conway on any vices, especially the more popular ones of the era. He had considered college, but drag racing was more important; his friends and family all knew this by now. His goals were to work, drag race, and become the best at the latter.

Conway went to work at E&B Transmissions in downtown Louisville, located on the corner of Preston and Breckinridge. "My job at the time was to remove transmissions, learn how to repair them, and install them after the repair," he said. "I was working with my friend Wimpy's brother, Chuck Christmas."

By now Conway could do engine builds on his own as well as clutch, suspension, and transmissions. "Other than what Wimpy and I taught Conway over the past few years, he was self-taught, a natural mechanic, and a natural engineer," said Tony. Conway's friends all knew he was brilliant; I wasn't surprised when I found out he had a high I.Q.; I could see it when he was just a kid.

As mentioned earlier in the book, Conway's I.Q. was extremely high, and researchers at Sociosite, Social Science Information Systems tell us that people with high I.Q.s have outstanding abilities in logical reasoning and can readily navigate complicated theoretical material. This was Conway, give him a problem, and he would solve it.

His intelligence would serve him well when it came to what he liked to do best, drag racing. It didn't always come easy, but the more he learned about the sport, the better he became. "In hindsight, I should have attended college and gotten an engineering degree," says Conway. "But I was a goofy kid and chose to follow my dream of professional drag racing."

In the summer of 1973, Conway partnered with friend Gary Buckley who owned a 1965 Mustang convertible. The car had a 289 four-speed. Using an engine Conway built with bargain parts from JC Whitney, a clutch Conway already had, and Gary's transmission, the pair raced the car heavily during the summer and fall. They had no trailer so the boys "flat towed," using another vehicle and a tow bar in order to get it to the Mustang to the races. Once there, they would remove the rear street tires from the Mustang and install a pair of racing slicks.

On Friday evenings they raced at U.S. 60 in Hardinsburg, Kentucky, then at Ohio Valley in Louisville on Saturday nights. On Sunday afternoon, they'd head to the drag strip in Elizabeth, Indiana.

"We learned all the ins and outs while traveling to three tracks every weekend. It was normal to break something, and we worked on our backs, lying in the grass with the bugs and 90-degree heat and humidity, fixing the clutch, trans, drive shaft, you name it." Conway went on to say that at one track there were two super stock levels, one for the experienced drivers and one for beginners. "I ran in the beginner's bracket and won many races!"

Conway and his partner raced throughout 1974, improving their driving, engine building, and money management skills.

In 1975 he changed jobs and went to work at Republic Diesel repairing and machining diesel cylinder heads. It was hot, miserable work, but he stuck with it and learned even more during this period. The partnership Mustang convertible was sold and Conway bought a 1964 Mustang hardtop. He built the engine and transmission, and set the whole car up for drag racing. He beat many faster cars and more experienced drivers with this home-built Mustang.

On the job, the whole crew at Republic loved racing and went to the drag races in the local area every weekend. Conway got to know them all, but the 19-year-old would have to face a bully for the first time in his life. Conway wasn't a tiny man; he was nearly six feet but slim at 160 pounds.

"There was a guy in the shop that started bullying me. He was bigger than me, but I wasn't scared of him. At first, I ignored him and went on about my work. This guy would tease me, called me names, he had a considerable attitude," said Conway.

One day the bully, Dennis, sprayed him down with an oil substance used on the heads to prevent rust. Conway hadn't done anything, but Dennis was arrogant and wanted to start trouble. Conway lost his temper and threw a punch; Dennis blocked the punch, but grabbed Conway's little finger, and snapped it like a twig.

After Conway completed surgery to correct the damage, and Dennis was reprimanded, management hoped transferring Conway to a counter job upfront would prevent further issues.

Not long after that incident, Conway was at the drag strip racing his Mustang. Most of the crew he worked with was there that night, and so was Dennis; he ran a Chevy gasser. At some point during the night, Dennis challenged Conway by driving behind him while staging.

This was a track procedure; you pulled up behind the car you wanted to race. Conway saw what was going on and remained in line. "There were at least 15 employees from our company there that evening, and they were mostly Dennis's friends," said Conway.

When it was their turn, the two men staged, the light went green, and at the finish line, it was Conway with the win. Dennis had to be embarrassed at this outcome; after all, he was more popular at work than Conway, and most of the guys came out to see him race.

Conway lines up for another race, and again, Dennis pulls in behind him. Both drivers stage, the light turns green, both drivers leave, and at the finish, Conway wins again.

"You know karma is real and Dennis got a huge taste of it that night," said Conway.

While racing the Mustang, Conway bought and raced a front engine dragster too.

"Few people remember the little front engine dragster Conway had in 1976," said long-time friend Leon Clark. Leon was Tony Clark's younger brother and first met Conway when he was 14 and Leon was 17. "We hung out a lot, and I helped him with several cars over the years," said Leon.

Conway bought an old top gas car from a local man and wanted to race it in the D/Econo Dragster class. The vehicle was a six-cylinder, 240 cubic inch Ford with a slipper clutch and side draft Weber carburetors.

"I painted the name "Tight Wad" on the side of the car because Conway only had nickels and dimes to spend on it. It was a real budget race car back then," said Leon.

A driver had to go through three qualifying sessions to receive a competition license. The sessions went from slow, then mid speed, then fast as track officials closely watched you.

"We took the car to Edgewater, Ohio, to get the license one weekend," said Leon. "Conway took the car down the track on its first pass with no problems, and the second was good too. Conway opened it up on the third pass and ran it as fast as possible.

At the end of the run, the announcer said, "Folks keep an eye on Conway Witten; this kid came within .25 hundred of a second of breaking the record in his class!"

"It was only his third run just to qualify for a license," said Leon. "I always knew Conway was special, but that day I was convinced he would have a great career in racing."

The rail lasted only a short time mainly because it needed to be faster for Conway, although he beat several V8 cars with it just fooling around. He sold the dragster and concentrated on the Mustang.

Sports Nationals May 28 through 31st, 1976
Beech Bend Drag Strip, Bowling Green Kentucky

Conway's first NHRA national event was the Sports Nationals in Bowling Green, Kentucky. "My friend David Walker owned a 1964 Comet and had it set up to race in Super Stock R," Conway said. "I built the engine in the car, a 289 four-barrel, and we towed it to the event on an open flatbed trailer with old Mercury David owned. We put all the tools, jacks, and spare parts into the trunk of the Mercury as well as the trunk of the Comet and headed for the event."

The car had to go through a NHRA technical inspection before being allowed to compete, and the rep identified a problem during the review. The rear wheel wells had been modified to get larger racing tires to fit.

The tech pointed this out using a colorful expression, "Looks like a hand grenade went off in the wells!" Sure enough, David had used a bumper jack to widen this area. After the inspection, the tech passed the car, and both men were surprised simply because of the issue with the wheel wells.

Conway said, "I figured the tech knew we were low budget and decided to let us compete even though we didn't have a chance. The wheel wells weren't a safety issue, and the car was in good shape other than that."

The car was cleared to race when a downpour started. The rain was so heavy that the track was partially underwater in no time. "We just stayed in the car talking about racing and waited out the storm," said Conway.

The track dried out the next day, and David got some qualifying runs in. He managed to qualify in the lower half of the competition, but in the first round, he got beaten significantly. Upset with himself and the car, David was ready to leave, and the two men loaded up and headed home to Louisville. David was so humiliated he never raced again. Conway, however, pulled the engine, took it home, and was extremely excited about the experience. "I thought this wasn't hard; I can do this!"

In June, Conway met a girl he completely fell for. Her name was Robin, and she was a real looker with a great personality. Conway took her everywhere; to the movies, out to eat, to the track while he was racing, and even to watch at other events he didn't run in. In fact, for the first time in his life, Conway limited his racing to spend more time with Robin. In his mind, they were in love. Robin and Conway celebrated their 21st birthdays together, only three weeks apart in age, but one night they had a bad argument over something trivial; after that, the relationship declined, and at the end of the year, they stopped seeing each other.

Conway still lived at home in the summer of 1976, using a basement bedroom to sleep in. One evening Conway came home from work and realized his father was missing from the dinner table. "Where's dad?" Conway asked his mother. She explained to Conway that Bill had checked himself into a local treatment facility.

The continuous arguing Bill and Wanda were having about his drinking had finally come to a climax. One family member physically confronted Bill about his drinking which resulted in him seeking help.

After spending a few weeks in treatment Bill returned home and went back to work. There was never any discussion about his treatment and Bill never drank another drop of alcohol the rest of his life.

The following year, 1977, Conway partnered with Mike Puckett using the same 1964 Mustang hardtop to race in Super Stock at the local tracks. This time the car was lettered 'Puckett & Witten.' To date, Conway had won several trophies and a small amount of cash and was having fun, but his goal remained the same; to be the best, and when the time was right, to be a professional. He was still learning the ins and outs of driving a race car and the business side of drag racing. He was learning from his mistakes and would soon learn a huge lesson from a mistake that could have taken his life.

Conway would experience four accidents during his twenty years as a drag racer, each event potentially killing him. The first occurred in June of 1977, and after a frightening few seconds, he wondered if it was all worth it.

Summer 1977, Ohio Valley Raceway

Conway does a burnout to heat the rear tires. He slowly approaches the staging area, brings the RPMS up in the 289 engine, the lights flash, and it's green; he dumps the clutch, launches off the line in first gear, after shifting into second he is dead even with his competitor, open headers roaring, Conway grabs third gear and gains a one car length lead, barely into fourth gear he crosses the finish and starts to brake, he has another win, another trophy.

But hold on, something's gone wrong, suddenly the car bucks and bounces in the air, then it comes back down on the track hard at 90 miles an hour, out of control, leaving the track, speeding into the weeds, finally coming to a stop.

His heart racing, Conway evaluates the situation. "I didn't hit anything, I didn't run into the other car, I'm out in the weeds, no fire, I'm not hurt, but holy smokes, I was in the air for a while!"

It took some time to figure out what happened, but when he did, he could only blame himself for the high-potential near miss he had just experienced.

"I had installed Chrome Molly traction bars on the car. It had what's known as a floating rear-end housing, and the floater made it dependent on the traction bar to hold it in place. I screwed up and installed the bars upside down," said Conway.

The bars probably broke when he launched in first gear; then they dug into the car's floor pan, which gave them enough support to hold during the run. When he let off the gas and applied the brakes at the end of the run, the bars came out of the floor pan and were jammed into the track surface. This action pulled the drive shaft out of the transmission, and the car pole vaulted over the shaft into the air, slamming down on the track and going out of control before stopping. He would learn a huge lesson that day: always follow installation instructions provided by the part manufacturer.

Spring of 1978

In late April of 1978, Conway was twenty-two years old, single, and doing some dating. His new girlfriend was from an affluent area of the city, and at first, Conway wasn't sure why she was interested in him, a working-class drag racing type. They were not serious, just hanging out together, taking long walks, going bowling, seeing a movie, and enjoying each other's company.

The week leading up to the Kentucky Derby, held on the first Saturday in May since 1875, is a huge party in the Louisville, Kentucky, area. Conway's girlfriend was invited to a Derby party, and she, in turn, asked Conway.

The couple arrived at the party and began mingling with the crowd, Conway felt uncomfortable. "These people were friends of my girl, not me. I had nothing in common with them; they were all high-class rich kids that had attended private schools, had new cars, had rich parents, and most were going to college somewhere. I felt out of place."

As the party went on, Conway sampled the punch, which tasted great. The host occasionally filled the bowl, and Conway started feeling better about the party.

The next thing he remembers is the following morning sitting in his car. "I woke up in my car sitting in my girlfriend's parent's driveway. I was covered in dried vomit; it was everywhere, inside my car and outside the passenger side. I felt like crap, and then I felt so embarrassed.

"What had I done? Who drove my car here? I had no memory of these things," Conway said.

Conway, a complete teetotaler, had been fooled in regards to the contents of the punch, which was filled with various brands of clear alcohol with taste-disguising fruit juices added. (In many circles, this type of gathering is called a "TKO Party. Before you know it, wham, the concoction sneaks up on you and you are "TKO," the acronym for a technical knockout.)

This type of punch would fool even an experienced drinker; no surprise it fooled Conway.

"I never went back to my girlfriends after that morning, I never called her, and she never called me. I was so embarrassed that I couldn't face her," Conway said. This was the first and last experience Conway ever had with alcohol. He also slept in and missed the derby completely.

Several years later, Conway ran into her at a church service. She told Conway that they were both plastered after drinking the special punch. Conway drove them back to her parent's home; she staggered into the house while Conway threw up on everything around it, including the shrubs.

She noticed Conway's health conditions, and he told her about his accident and his near-death experience. She was the first person to suggest that his story should be documented somehow, a short story, or maybe a book.

In November of 1978 Conway decided to buy a new car, a daily driver. He selected his new car from Doublemont Chevrolet in Louisville, owned by brothers Rich and

Bob Montgomery. The car, a dark blue 1979 Corvette, right off the showroom floor, was equipped with a 350 cubic inch V8 and automatic transmission, it had all the options.

Life for Conway was getting interesting. He just celebrated his 23 birthday, had a great job, a new Corvette, was building a new race car, and had a new girlfriend. Her name was Jackie. She was the receptionist for the company he worked at.

"I can only imagine what people thought when they would see me in the Corvette with Jackie in the passenger seat. She was a beautiful blond," said Conway. He was about to get a lesson in relationships that he would never forget.

There was a customer that was frequented the parts department routinely, his name was Bill Fleker. Fleker was a racing engine builder and racer, Conway knew him from the drag strip. He would come in a couple of times a week to buy parts and always ended up talking to Conway. During most of these conversations he would mention Jackie, "She's pretty," "How old is she?" "Does she date anyone?" Conway finally told him that yes, he and Jackie were dating. "I didn't think much about it at first," said Conway. Fleker asked Conway out to lunch a few times and one day told him about his niece, "She's really pretty, you should ask her out." This occurred several times and Conway always turned him down.

One weekend Jackie decided to go to a rock concert with an old boyfriend and didn't tell Conway about it until after it happened. Although she said it was just a chance to see the Rolling Stones for free, and that nothing had occurred during the date, Conway was still upset. Upset enough to take Fleker up on his offer the next time he mentioned his niece.

Fleker's niece by marriage, Carla Pace, worked two jobs at the time, one at a general store in the area and another one at a large auto parts warehouse through the week.

Conway got Carla's number and called her. He explained who he was and that her uncle had suggested he call. After some small talk, Carla agreed on a date, even though she had never seen him in person, for the following Saturday night.

With that, Conway decided to go on a small stealth mission. He knew where the general store was so the following Saturday morning he went in to check Carla out.

"I knew most of the folks that came in the store, they lived in the area and I had been working there since I was thirteen, "said Carla.

"I saw this guy come in that I didn't recognize. He bought a coke, a candy bar, and some M&M's. He had a kind smile and looked directly in my eyes, but he never said a word, just paid and left. I watched him leave; he was driving a new blue Corvette."

Later that evening, Carla was getting ready for her 'blind' date. When Conway came up to the door, she immediately recognized him, but she didn't mention it at first. They introduced themselves to each other and walked to the car. Conway opened the door and Carla got in. Once seated, she turned to Conway and said, "Well, did I pass the test?" He acted like he didn't know what she was talking about. "You came in the store today to check me out, didn't you? Carla said. Conway was embarrassed but said nothing. Carla noticed the M&M's sitting on the console and held them up. "Where did you get these from?" Conway knew he was busted! "Do you still want to go out," Conway asked? Carla said yes, but she told him she didn't like games.

They went to dinner and talked the entire time. They found each other interesting and agreed to go out again. Over the next week, Conway saw Carla two more times, it seemed like a natural fit to him when they were together.

Later that week while at work he found jackie crying. Conway approached her and asked what was wrong. "Bill Fleker called me; he said you were seeing his niece and wanted to know if I wanted to go out with him. I told him no way." She burst into tears, and Conway started apologizing. "I was mad about your date and thought you were getting back with your old boyfriend." Conway realized Bill had set him up; he had been after Jackie.

The couple made up, and Conway decided to end the short-time relationship with Carla immediately. He stopped calling her and wouldn't return her calls. Did Carla know what was really going on?

By the end of the year, Conway's racing partnership with Mike Puckett had ended, so he partnered with another friend, Jim Powers.

The new partnership would build a Mustang race car from scratch using a donated body. Powers and Witten built the shell of the 1964 Mustang hardtop into a formidable super stock racer during the winter of 1979.

The car featured a 289 engine built by Conway from the ground up, a heavy-duty four-speed transmission, a modern full race suspension, and a roll cage; it was a purpose-built car.

In the middle of the build, Conway went to work for Snap-on Tools, a company that manufactured their line of mechanics tools from A to Z and other products used in the mechanic's realm. He had a new two-ton Van supplied by the company and an established sales route, although Conway sought out new customers too. Once the Mustang was finished, Jim and Conway took it out for its first shakedown run at a track in Louisville.

"I was at the track the day Conway took the new Mustang for its first run," said Chuck Belanger, one of Conway's lifelong friends. "He came off the line hard and made a great pass, only one small issue. They had sandblasted the car during the building stage, and during the first run, sand was pouring out of the car from several places. It was on track, in the air, quite a mess!"

The first racing event the partners attended was out of state in the early spring. Heavy rain delayed the races, and the pair spent the night in the Mustang. The next day it continued to rain, and the boys decided to go home. Just outside Louisville, they ran into an ice storm, and the roads were dangerously slick, but they made it home without incident.

Although the car performed well early on, it started breaking parts at practically every event they went to. "It was a little of everything, but it was constant," said Conway. The partners had a string of bad luck in the summer of 1979, which was frustrating for them.

The following year Jim and Conway were attempting to race the Mustang again in a super stock class. Early in 1980, they had a few wins, and the car was running great, but Conway's relationship with Jackie was heading south.

"She loved to party, drink, drugs, the whole works; I wasn't into that and tried to get her to stop. It was aggravating because I liked her," said Conway.

CHAPTER 3

CARLA, CORVETTES, AND NATIONAL RECORDS
1980 to 1983

May of 1980 would bring several changes to Conway's life. The first was breaking up with Jackie because of her vices; it was just too much for him. This hurt, but it had to be done. The next event in his life was even worse.

One night Conway pulled the Snap-on Tool truck up to the house and shut the engine off. It had been a long day, and Conway had been trying hard to collect some debts owed him. He was almost a year into this job and was having second thoughts about his future in this profession. Just as he walked into the house, the phone rang.

"Conway," a female voice said. "I have bad news for you," A few minutes later, Conway hung the phone up and sat down; tears rolling down his cheeks.

Earlier that day, Conway's racing partner, Jim Powers, picked up his nephew on his motorcycle and headed for a ride on a rural Kentucky road. During the trip, he lost control of the bike, ran off the paved road, and crashed, killing both men instantly.

Early in the month Conway learned that Carla had not been a part of her uncle's plan to steal his former girlfriend. He was relieved, and decided to surprise her with flowers and a card.

"I was at work one day when a vase of flowers and a card were delivered to me. I opened the card and it said 'From a long lost lover.' I wasn't dating anyone at the time and couldn't figure it out," said Carla. As she walked out of the building there stood Conway, next to Corvette. She was carrying the flowers and asked him if they were from him, he said they were. They started dating again.

Carlotta Ann Pace was born in Valley Station on the south side of Louisville, Kentucky, on March 4, 1960, to Harden and Barbara Pace. The oldest of three children, she had a sister and brother in that order.

Her father was an auto and truck mechanic and worked at his father's full-service gas station, Pace's Phillip 66. Barbara was a stay-at-home mom during her children's formative years, but when they got older, she worked at a junior high school cafeteria, where she became the manager.

Carlotta was a pretty girl, brunette, with a warm smile and friendly manner. She loved outdoor sports, ran track, kept stats for the baseball team, and loved music. Carla learned piano as a child and sang in the high school choir. She was a cheerleader in grade school and received good grades throughout her school years. Due to her grades in high school, she was invited to join the Beta Club, an academic honors program with a strong emphasis on community service. The Beta Club members' aim is to promote the ideals of character and academic achievement.

When asked what attracted her to Conway, she said, "He was fun to talk to, spontaneous and motivated."

When asked what attracted Conway to Carla he said, "She was beautiful, smart, and funny.

Conway decided to leave Snap-on Tools and took a job with Colortech, a North American-based manufacturer of color and additive concentrates for the plastics industry. An office in Louisville provided recruiting support for the factory located in Overland Park, Kansas. After two weeks of training, Conway began traveling around the US, interviewing prospective employees and eventually hiring them for the company.

The entire summer and early fall of 1980 was nothing but travel, and it cut into his racing and personal life. Now, every spare moment he had was with Carla, not the race car. They were becoming very close, and while on a trip to Texas, Conway knew he was in love with her.

On a warm August night, Conway proposed to Carla and she happy accepted. They planned the wedding for January of the following year. Conway made the engagement official in September by presenting her with a ring. They attended a portion of the NHRA US Nationals in Indianapolis, but Conway wasn't racing; he was there to watch a friend compete in the Competition Eliminator class.

January 17th, 1981

Conway, now 26 years old, married Carla Pace, 21, in a large Church wedding on Saturday, January 17, 1981. Carla's dress, homemade by her mother and maternal grandmother, the material provided by her parental grandmother, was beautiful, and both families, including a large gathering of friends, attended the wedding at the South Jefferson Baptist Church and the reception at the Sun Valley Country Club. Neither Conway nor Carla was interested in a formal honeymoon, so the couple spent the weekend at the historic Galt House, a swanky hotel on the riverfront in Louisville, Kentucky.

The newly married Witten couple first lived in an apartment in the Louisville area. Carla worked two jobs, and Conway was now working for an industrial supply company as a traveling salesman. The couple decided to work hard and save for a house. They both agreed that having children this early in the marriage wasn't the best idea. Carla wanted to return to school, and Conway wanted to continue racing.

Shortly after their marriage, Conway lost his job. The company he was working for went out of business, and there was little notice given to the employees. The couple made some quick decisions about their finances and decided to sell a few things they could do without. It was a humbling experience for both of them when Conway put the Corvette, the ski boat, and his Harley motorcycle up for sale. It didn't take Conway long to find another job, and the couple moved on.

The couple enjoyed music, and listening to new and older selections in their collection was always fun. Conway had an expensive stereo system, and the music always had an excellent sound.

The Mustang had been mainly sitting idle since the death of Conway's partner the previous year, and he was looking for more of a challenge. He wanted to upgrade to a faster class and change cars. In the spring, he sold the Mustang and started looking for another car to race. By July, he found one, a big block Corvette already set up. "I had the car's owner meet me at the Bowling Green, Kentucky drag strip," Conway said. "I wanted to see the car run under track conditions. The owner had numerous problems that day, but I saw enough to know I wanted it."

Conway bought the car with the money he had from selling the other Corvette; he took it home that day.

The 1970 Corvette was a 454 V8 with 365 horses and an automatic transmission. The NHRA class it ran in was Super Stock H, and Conway had big plans for it. Over the next few weekends, Conway pulled the engine and disassembled it piece by piece, paying extra attention to the heads; he knew how to make the engine produce more horsepower. That was one of Conway's unique skills, knowing how far he could squeeze all the horsepower and torque out of the 454 and still be legal under the rules set by the NHRA.

In addition to the engine work, the transmission was modified with a shift kit and cooler, and the suspension and rear end remained untouched for now. After testing the new modifications, Conway was ready for some competition.

Saturday, August 8, 1981

Conway took the Corvette to Bunker Hill, Indiana, drag strip, where a points race event was being held. After beating all the competition in his class and on the last run of the day, he hit a milestone in his racing career: setting a record in his class, the first of many to come. It was a track record and a national record in one of the most competitive classes in Super Stock. The rules stated that for the national record to be official, the engine and the car had to pass a technical inspection, which involved including removing the intake and heads from the engine. Conway passed the inspection, loaded the car on the trailer, and headed home.

Carla joined him at the races as much as she could in the early days of their marriage. She learned how to help with specific tasks over the first few months, and one day she wanted to show her husband she could load the race car on the trailer.

Conway had an open flatbed car hauler with a winch installed to pull the car on with. The winch came in handy if the car broke down, but it was also necessary because of the car's low stance. The doors would hit the trailer wheel well covers once on the trailer, so the driver couldn't get out. The winch handle had three positions and could confuse a newcomer, but Carla had the task down cold, or so she thought.

One afternoon in Nashville, Tennessee, Carla was operating the winch to load the car up for the trip home.

The pulling vehicle and trailer were sitting on a slight grade, and once the car was loaded, Carla put the winch in neutral instead of park. Suddenly the race car began rolling backward. It rolled off the trailer and was gaining speed.

Once the winch cable was fully extended, it didn't hold and snapped under the weight and momentum of the car. The racecar starts going even faster, rolling backward, passing people, vehicles, other race cars, and trailers. The car rolled off the road and smacked into some trees, coming to a stop. No one was hurt, and the race car had only minor damage.

On the way home that night, it was apparent that Conway was upset. He kept asking Carla, "How could you do something like that?" She apologized and told him she would never operate the winch again. "That's for sure," remarked Conway.

Sunday, October 25, 1981

Conway's longtime friend, Chuck Belanger, was once again a crew member helping him with his race car. The pair traveled to Bluegrass Raceway in Lexington, about 75 miles from home.

Conway was getting his wish with faster times because the Corvette was traveling the quarter mile in ten seconds at 130 mph, much faster than his Mustang had.

Due to the flat bottom oil pan design, purposely used to increase horsepower, less oil than average was used in the engine, creating a situation where Conway would have to shift the car into neutral at the end of each run to keep from damaging the engine. Conway ran the car several times down the track perfecting this procedure with no issues.

Later that day, Conway was in the lanes behind a '69 427 Camaro that had just left the lights. The driver, Irvin Thackett, was hauling down the track when suddenly, as he entered neared the finish line the car wobbled from side to side, stopping at the end of the track. The transmission had blown up at the end of the run, and debris had penetrated the floorboard, striking the driver in both legs. The ambulance was dispatched and took the driver to the hospital, and without an ambulance, racing had to stop until it returned.

Chuck and Conway continued to check and prep the Corvette; once the ambulance returned, Conway won several races. On his next run, he entered the water box and did a burnout; the car felt strong, and he was staged and ready to take on the next challenger.

"When the light turned green, I hit the gas, lifting the front wheels slightly off the ground. I hit each shift point perfectly, and at the end of the run, the engine was turning at 8,000 RPMs, "Conway continued. "I hit the kill button, and when I shifted into neutral, I heard a loud bang and immediately felt a horrible pain in my right foot. I used my left foot to brake and hit the pedal as hard as possible. It seemed like it took ten minutes to get the car stopped, and at that time, the pain was driving me out of my mind. I stopped in the middle of the lane, rolled out of the car, hobbled away, and lay on the pavement, twisting and crying in pain."

Chuck ran down the track towards Conway, screaming, "Are you alright?' An EMT got to him first and asked where he was hurt. Conway told him his right foot, and as the EMT pulled off his shoe, one of his toes fell to the ground, and blood was everywhere. The EMTs immediately knew another transmission had exploded and loaded Conway in the ambulance. Dave Embry, another friend of Conway's, was also there, and he was recruited to carry the toe to the hospital.

Conway was hospitalized and given a saddle block to numb his body from the waist down. The doctor could not reattach the amputated toe and removed potions of two other damaged toes. Conway was sleeping when Carla arrived, and she was crying by his bedside when he woke up.

Conway identified the cause of the explosion once he was home and could investigate it. The valve body in the transmission was defective. Another lesson learned and the second accident he had experienced since he started racing. There would be two more.

1982

The year 1982 would be a very busy one for both Conway and Carla. Carla wanted to continue her education. In high school, she had been a "Candy Striper" at a local hospital in the Louisville area, so medicine seemed like a good place to start.

She attended Spencerian College, first taking and passing a Nursing Assistant course. "I attended the classes at night and remained working," Carla commented. Her goal was to become a registered nurse.

Conway would meet two essential people that year; both men were named Mike.

The first Mike was Mike Keown. Conway had known of him before 1982 because he was a drag racer and ran an engine-building business. Keown, a machinist, and student of well-known John Lingenfelter (owner of Lingenfelter Engineering, specializing in Corvette and Firebird performance engines and parts), was a legend in the drag racing community. Keown had been racing since the 1960s and was known nationwide for the quality racing engines he built. He had invented some innovative racing parts at the time, including a lightweight wrist pin, a component used to connect the rod to the piston, and a carburetor adapter. Mike had been watching Conway at the drag strip and realized his skills as an engine builder, especially the custom work he did on cylinder heads. He invited Conway to work for him, putting him in charge of all the head work in the shop. Conway was now part of a team that built engines for people all over the US and Canada used for drag racing, stock car racing, truck, and tractor pulling; it was competition racing, they built the engines.

The second "Mike" was Mike Farrell. Mike was a drag racer, too, and also a co-owner with his father, C.J., in a large trucking company known simply as Farrell

Trucking. The company specialized in hauling hazardous chemicals and did business with companies nationwide. Mike recognized Conway's intelligence and offered him a job as the second shift dispatcher which later turned into a manager position.

Conway, still very young at 26 was now working from 9 am to 3:30 pm at Keown's engine building shop and from 4 pm to midnight at Ferrell Trucking, two important jobs with tons of responsibility.

The Witten couple also purchased their first home that year, just a short distance from Conway's old neighborhood; they were now in the Pleasure Ridge Park section of Louisville. The house had two bedrooms, an oversized two-car garage, and a full basement.

Carla continued to work at a large hot rod auto parts warehouse called 'Action Automotive,' the wholesale distributor for the Grand Automotive Company based in Chicago. In addition, she still worked at a general store part-time. She also worked part-time as a home interior salesperson, holding parties at prospective customer homes demonstrating different home décor. She also made and sold crafts, specifically floral arrangements, and jewelry, on a seasonal basis.

In drag racing, sometimes racers help their friends and competitors in need. There are several examples of Conway giving back to people at the track when they needed help. In the following example, Mike Keown and Conway are mentioned for their good deeds.

The following was posted on a drag racing website by Mike Pearson from Tampa, Florida. "I did some serious damage to my engine while racing at Bowling Green one weekend. Mike and Conway volunteered their time and energy and we pulled the engine after Conway found us a place that would work.

They took my engine to Mike's shop and rebuilt it. Conway did the headwork while Mike honed the block. They worked through the day and night. Starting at 10 in the morning and finishing at eight the following morning. I put the engine back in the car and raced."

Now completely healed from his racing accident, Conway decided to take advantage of an NHRA rule change specifically for Corvettes.

From the factory, Corvettes came with had an independent rear suspension, the differential housing only holds the ring gear and differential carrier. The axle housing is mounted into the vehicle with the use of what's known as a cradle. This cradle is also where the control arms of the rear suspension mount. This type of suspension results in a smoother all around ride but is weaker under the strain of constant torque. Conway was breaking numerous parts in the rear suspension to the point of body damage in one case and the rule change allowed him to install a straight axle suspension more suitable for drag racing.

After the rear-end modifications and the quarter panels were repaired, Conway set two more national records with the car in his class; breaking his own record, he was ready for the US Nationals.

September 1, 1982, NHRA US Nationals, Indianapolis, Indiana

Conway and his team traveled to Indianapolis for the 27th running of the NHRA US Nationals. He was celebrating his 27th birthday just a few weeks later and he felt this was good luck. This would be his very first appearance at the nationals as a driver, and he was about to make history!

The NHRA US Nationals is considered the most prestigious drag racing event in the world due to its history, size, and purse. Drag racers from all over the US and the world come to this event to test their cars and driving skills against the best in the world.

The first US Nationals event was held Labor Day weekend, 1955, at the Great Bend Municipal Airport in Great Bend, Kansas. In 1961 the event was held in Indianapolis and has remained at this venue ever since.

There were 23 entries in Super Stock H automatic at the 1982 nationals. The favorite was Charlie Graf, who raced a 1967 small-block Camaro. Graf's car was a former John Lingenfelter car that featured all the latest technology and was fast. Graft was the defending champion and knew the car Conway was driving from the previous owner, but he didn't know the engine builder, Conway.

When qualifying in the class completed, Conway was number one with a 10:52 elapsed time in the quarter mile. Everyone else was running 10:65 through 10:89, and they were a little angry at the youngster and his car. Rumors were circulating that Conway was cheating or he had spent enormous amounts of money trying to buy his way to the winner's circle. But when the tire smoke cleared, the final round consisted of Charlie Graf's Camaro and Conway Witten's Corvette. Twenty-one other cars had been defeated; the stage was set!

"In the left lane, Conway Witten from Louisville, Kentucky, in his Corvette going up against the defending class champion in the right lane, Charlie Graf from Munchkin, New Jersey, in his '67 Camaro." The announcer at the nationals ended the introductions, and the two men did their water box burnouts. Both men staged, and the lights on the Christmas tree started the countdown.

Both drivers get a good start, and the cars are almost even; at half-track, the Corvette pulls ahead, and at the finish, it's Conway Witten with the win, running a 10:51 against Graf's 10:62. Conway is the winner with a ten-second run at over 130 mph in the quarter mile. Conway, a 26-year-old, self-taught mechanic, built the engine, the transmission, and the suspension using budget parts and highly skilled hands.

Graf is angry as he storms over to Conway's pit, where he immediately recognizes Mike Keown among the others that came to watch Conway run. "I spent over $110,000 to come here and kick ass. Then you show up in THAT THING!" Charlie screams at no one in particular while pointing at Conway's car. Charlie has his fingers crossed while hoping Conway is cheating and will fail the tech inspection.

The NHRA technical inspection will prove otherwise, however, and Conway's win is official. But there did turn out to be one small problem...

In his first appearance at the U.S. Nationals, Conway won his class and received his first "Wally," the nick name for the class winning trophy, named after Wally Parks, the founder of the NHRA....with a cracked block!

1983

1983 is a repeat of the previous year. Very few can compete with him in his class, and he wins the US Nationals for the second year. It was a good racing year with one exception: Most Camaro owners were complaining about Conway's engine setup. It wasn't illegal but there was complaint after complaint. Conway put on his "thinking cap" one day after the nationals.

In October, he told his friend Kenny Morris, "If I take the 454 out and replace it with a 350 small block, I could run in Super Stock I automatic." Running a 350 would put him at the same weight break as the Camaros, and the king of Super Stock I was Dick Henry out of Morehead, North Carolina, in his red 1967 Camaro.

"My goal was to break the national record in this class, too," said Conway.

Conway had a 350 V8 engine, and he tore it down and massaged it with his unique touch. He installed it in the Vette, intending to take the car to Suffolk, Virginia, in November.

One minor issue was experienced after the new motor installation; an oil pan was borrowed and it rubbed on the steering drag link tube while turning left or right. Since drag racing is a straight-down-the-track sport, it shouldn't be an issue, but he had to be careful.

The track at Suffolk was perfect for setting national records because it was at sea level and had the best possible air; plus, the racing surface was concrete for better traction.

"My boss at the trucking company, Mike Ferrell, financed the trip with one request. He wanted to drive my car in competition at least once" Conway agreed, and off they went to Virginia in early November.

The first run was given to Mike; but he over-revved the engine during the burnout and broke a valve spring. When the race started, he pulled the wheels off the ground, and when they came down, the drag link rubbed, causing the car to come a little out of the groove. He drove the car back to the pit and shut it off. "I'm not driving this car again," said Mike, visibly scared.

Conway removed the valve covers, repaired the broken spring, adjusted the valves on both sides and climbed in behind the wheel.

On Conway's first run, he went 10:41, beating Dick Henry's best time of 10:43 and setting a new record.

CHAPTER 4
GOING AFTER THE HEMI'S
1984 -1986

The following year Conway was winning practically everywhere he went. He once again qualified and made it to the final round in his class at the 1984 US Nationals. This year he screwed up and red-lighted.

"I have some great memories of Conway and the Corvette from back in the day," said Leon Clark. "When Conway bought the Corvette, it was two-tone silver and black. He would pull into the local tracks with the Vette on an open trailer, and soon his competition would load up and leave. Leon was at a local track one day ahead of Conway, sitting in the pits waiting for him. When Conway pulled in, Leon heard another racer say, "Well, that cuts it; I'm leaving; I can't beat that guy!" No one wanted to face the Vette; Conway was too fast and consistent." Leon went on to say that Conway devised a plan to keep his competition from leaving early.

The plan was to paint the car differently, and he chose Monza Red, an actual GM color for Corvettes. "That paint job was good for one visit per track back then" laughed Leon. "Once the competition learned it was still Conway, they started packing up and leaving again!"

One night Conway told Leon that he felt the front end of the Vette was getting light at the top end. After another run, Conway was convinced that this was happening. The two men studied the situation and did some testing. Sure enough at the top end, the air coming in through the opening under the grill (the grill was closed off by the factory) was trapped under the hood long enough to cause this effect. This time it was Leon who came up with a solution. "Let's raise the back of the hood a few inches so the air can escape faster," suggested Leon. The rear of the hood was raised, and the problem was solved.

Carla continued her education and applied for Nursing School at Bellarmine University, where she was accepted. Unfortunately, the cost of the tuition was more than the couple could afford.

She then went on to a community college to get some introductory courses out of the way on a part-time basis while still working. Her goal was to get a degree, and she was adamant about finishing.

"We were both still young, working very hard, and making sacrifices," said Carla. "We discussed the tuition and came up with another plan for my education. I wanted Conway to keep racing because he was driven and sure of himself. The only problem we had was spending time together, and we didn't have any. I was going one way Conway was going another, and I missed spending quality time with him."

Conway and Carla had end goals to meet, and both thought they could meet each other's needs and maintain their goals.

1985

In 1985, the NHRA drag racing classes of Super Stock A, B, and C, were dominated by Hemi engine cars. It was racing territory that Chevy and Ford guys typically stayed away from. But Conway was looking for a new challenge for his Corvette.

So, during the winter of 1985 he put together a plan for his Corvette to race in the Super Stock B Automatic class. The engine he would use would be 454 cubic inches producing 465 horses in stock form, rated by the NHRA at 500 horses, the same as the Hemi.

"Why not go after those Hemi cars?" Conway thought.

The Chrysler Hemi engines, known by the trademark "Hemi, "are a series of American V8 gasoline engines built by Chrysler with overhead valve hemispherical combustion chambers. Chrysler has built three different types of Hemi engines for automobiles: the first known as the Chrysler Fire Power engine from 1951 to 1958, the second from 1964 to 1971, and the third beginning in 2003."

The first Hemi was 331 cubic inches, and it progressed from there. The famous 354 and 392 cubic-inch Hemi engines were found on the drag strip in the early days in practically every application from stock to super stock, all the way to top fuel. The overall design of the engine was popular due to the hemispherical shape that allowed for more volume at the top of the piston.

This creates more combustion, which produces more horsepower. The second-generation Hemi engine came in a 426 cubic inch package, which dominated drag racing in Stock, Super Stock, Pro-Stock, A/FX - Funny Cars, and top fuel. History shows they were hard to beat in a drag race and on the NASCAR circuit.

In 2003 Chrysler introduced the third-generation Hemi which impacted the value of first and second-generation Hemi-equipped cars, pushing prices up to six figures and beyond. Five factories' Hemi-equipped cars are currently in the top ten of the most expensive "American Muscle Cars" ever sold at auction.

The following Hemi cars are listed in order of their place in the top ten.

#3 -1971 Hemi' Cuda Convertible- 3.5 million, #4- 1970 Hemi 'Cuda Convertible-2.7 million, #5-1970 Hemi Challenger Convertible-1.4 million, #6-'69 Hemi Daytona-1.3 million, #8-1971 Hemi 'Cuda Convertible-1.1 million

Conway built his own engines, and this one was no exception. From the block to the heads, the crankshaft, and the cam, this engine was balanced, blueprinted, and had nothing but the best parts. It would be one of the best he had ever built.

He was about to make history!

Conway was a very hard worker, and was still working two jobs. Fortunately, at the engine building shop, he was allowed time to work on his own builds. Conway took his time on this build to ensure the engine was high-performance.

Throughout the first half of 1985, Conway prepared the Corvette for the new class. He beefed up the rear suspension and overhauled the automatic transmission; not one inch of the car was overlooked.

He took the car to Beechbend Raceway Park in Bowling Green, Kentucky, in late August. "I went there to test the car but beat everyone I raced," said Conway. My next stop was the nationals.

Meanwhile, after completing a year at the community college, Carla was accepted at the J.B. Speed Engineering School at the University of Louisville and began computer programming courses, but soon realized she preferred to have more personal interaction with others, and moved to the main school to pursue a degree in education.

August 30 – September 2, 1985, NHRA US Nationals, Indianapolis, Indiana

Conway traveled 117 miles from Louisville to Indy for the 30th Annual NHRA US Nationals, affectionately known as "The Big Go." He aimed to dispatch as many Hemi-powered Plymouth and Dodges as possible.

"I felt like the Hemi drivers were too cocky about their dominance in the Super Stock classes. I told my friends privately that my goal with this car was to beat them all if I could," said Conway. In addition, he had a written message for the Hemi driver, and in his opinion, it was located in the proper place so all the Hemi drivers could read it. A slogan on the rear license plate of the Witten Corvette read as follows; "Evil-Wicked -Mean and Nasty." Conway knew the slogan well, it was from a 1960s Steppenwolf song.

Conway's closest friends will tell you that he wasn't arrogant about his skills as a car and engine builder or even a driver. They saw confidence and determination, a young man living a dream and making the most of his limited resources.

The Corvette was producing 698 horses at the flywheel, and 600 foot-pounds of torque. He could feel every bit of it when he launched because keeping the front wheels on the ground was challenging.

Once again, Conway was about to make history at the most prestigious venue in drag racing. The field of cars in the Super Stock B Automatic class was numerous, requiring him to go four rounds before reaching the finals. Could he do it?

The crowd was almost silent watching his Chevy take down "The Fire-Breathing King of the Track" Hemi powered cars one by one.

The cat calls coming from the crowd that weekend were intense. "He's cheating!" "Check him for NOS," "That POS Chevy must be cheating," "That Hillbilly Boy is hiding something." The Hemi drivers were confused as well. "How can this guy beat all those Hemi cars round after round," questioned one Hemi fan?

The finals for SS/BA at the Nationals in 1985 featured future NHRA Hall of Fame inductee Steve Bagwell, from Norcross, Georgia, in his strong running 1965 Dodge A990 lightweight 426 Hemi facing Louisville, Kentucky's own Conway Witten and self built budget 454 Corvette, with no sponsors.

The race was on, and the big Hemi car took off like a thoroughbred horse on steroids, pulling the wheels off the ground, with flames shooting from the open headers. Bagwell was on his game that night, making his shift points, driving hard, and determined to win. But Conway had other ideas, and at the finish the red Corvette from Kentucky was ahead of the Hemi with an ET of 9.47 at 139.5 mph.

He had done it! Conway had just defeated five Hemi-powered cars to win the "Wally" at the US Nationals in SS/BA, and his best ET was faster than all 17 Hemi cars that had competed in the class.

One of the largest crowds in history waited nervously while NHRA officials completed the required technical inspected of Witten's Corvette. The majority of the crowd were Hemi fans, and were certain the "Hillbilly Boy" from Kentucky and his "POS" red Corvette were illegal in some way.

After thoroughly inspecting the car, much to the disappointment of the MOPAR fans everywhere, it was official: NHRA staff declared Conway, the winner. He would soon earn a new nick name.

After this amazing feat, and still without a sponsor, Conway set a new two-way record in both ET and MPH in his class.

Conway had just celebrated his 30th birthday, and was already looking ahead to what else could be accomplished in drag racing with the red Corvette.

Little did he know that the following season would bring a new experience in the form of NHRA politics; it would change his direction in the sport.

Unknown to Conway, General Motors representatives had watched his drag racing progress. They liked what they saw with the Corvette and were looking for good drivers and engine builders to take on their Oldsmobile Cutlass program. The plan was simple; GM would give the selected person a new Olds two-door G body car.

The recipient was required to use a shop they had already contracted to prepare the car for drag racing, they couldn't license the car for street use, and they had to race with a GM engine. There would be no other funding. Conway was contacted, and the program was explained to him. While thinking it over, the only hurdle for him was using the shop that GM had chosen.

Of course Conway wanted to do the work himself, along with a fabricator he knew in Louisville. Conway called GM with his counteroffer. This caused a series of phone calls to occur between several different people over the next few days. Eventually, GM agreed to his request; the car would be ready to pick up later that fall. Could this be the big break Conway had been looking for? This could lead to significant sponsors and a chance at full-time professional racing at a higher level, maybe even Pro Stock.

1986

At the beginning of 1986, both Conway and Carla were extremely busy. He was still working two jobs, and Carla was working and going to college, scheduled to graduate in the spring. "I went to school part-time and worked full-time as long as possible. I then switched and went to full-time school and part-time work," said Carla. She took a part-time job at Frito Lay and packed bags of chips into boxes from 11 pm to 6 am, then went home, ate, showered, and attended classes from 8 am to 3 pm. She would then go home and try to get some sleep before going back to work at 11 pm.

"Conway and I saw very little of each other during this time, but we were both motivated with specific goals." Although the pay was good at Frito Lay, Carla was exhausted most of the time, and after one semester of that schedule, she went looking for another job, and found a part time evening job at a local bank.

Conway was at the top of his game, an exceptional racing engine builder; welder, fabricator, and designer. His driving skill behind the wheel of practically any race car, manual or automatic transmission, was excellent. Most people do not realize the skill and athleticism it takes to race a high-performance car on a drag strip.

Besides the philosophy of staging, the driver must develop quick reflexives regarding the starting line, the best RPMs to launch with, and the tendencies of the car's setup at the start, mid-track, and shutdown.

There is much to know if you want to be the best in your class. It takes hours and hours of testing and experimenting with new parts, including tires, clutch, rear-end ratios, carburetors, electrical systems, fuels, and carburetors.

"Conway was exceptional at budgeting his money and time, resulting in a winning combo," said Bob Toy, a drag racer himself and friend to Conway. "He would have made one heck of a Corporate leader had he chosen that direction."

Winning drivers like Conway know their cars inside and out. The other challenges in drag racing are the weather and track conditions. Extreme cold or hot temps call for different tuning and suspension adjustments, tire air pressure, and sometimes fuel mixtures. The track altitude comes into consideration too. The closer to sea level you bring, the best air mixture to the engine, and higher altitudes may take a different engine tune. Although Conway was not a full-time racer, he competed against them, and to-date, he has beaten some of the best. Another skill Conway brings to the table is money management. He can squeeze more horsepower out of his engines on a meager budget, a skill he also uses on the rest of the car.

After Conway defeated the Hemi cars at the Nationals, a popular nationally published magazine, Super Stock, whose first issue was released in 1964, sent a representative to Conway's home in early 1986 to write an article about him and his Corvette. The title of the piece, once completed, said it all in just four bold words, HEMI-EATING CORVETTE – ASSASSIN, by Reno Zavagon.

Reno writes in his early 1986 article, "Conway Witten has the competition shaking its collective heads at his surprising Super Stock Corvette.

In a class infested with Hemis, the SS/BA Chevrolet has run faster than most SS/AA cars- how bout 9.40's on a 10'05 index?"

It was true; Conway was going faster in his class than most of cars in the next higher class, also dominated by Hemis. Reno went to the heart of the article's subject. Was the Corvette legal?

"Since Conway Witten's Corvette has become a serious threat in SS/BA, several questions have been raised concerning the legality of the exceptional machine."

Reno explained that the car was indeed legal under current NHRA rules. The Hemi competitors disagreed and cited the LS-7 option in the Corvette as being rare and questionable.

Conway was running a cast iron CZL block, not an aluminum block, he was even running cast iron heads, again, not aluminum. Rumors were to the contrary, but it just wasn't so. Conway was legal under the existing rules.

The final paragraph in Reno's article came true in a sense, was it a prediction, or did Reno know more than he was willing to share? "It seems that more controversy will surround the car when campaigned in the future, but at this point, it appears to be no stopping NHRA's quickest Super Stock Chevrolet from becoming even quicker."

In March of 1986, Conway traveled to the NHRA Motor Craft Gator-Nationals in Gainesville, Florida, and picked up where he left off. He again defeated the field of hemi-powered A and B-bodied cars and took home the class wins in SS/BA.

Shortly after his win a large group of the SS/B Hemi owners filed a protest with the NHRA against Conway's Corvette. Their protest stated that Conway's engine in his Corvette, the LS7, had never been made available for sale to the general public. Conway got the official notice from the NHRA informing him that the protest was under review, which was confusing because, for the past 16 years, there was language in the NHRA rule book identifying this combination. The engine was factored at 500 horsepower for competition purposes. The NHRA ignored his attempt to appeal under this fact after they sided with the Hemi drivers. His Corvette was officially banned from running in SS/BA.

It looked to a disappointed Conway that the NHRA had given in to the Chrysler Hemi crowd and the Chrysler Corporation.

The MOPAR fans were a vast and popular group; as was the Chrysler Corporation.

Conway didn't want to fight "City Hall," so to speak; he just wanted to race. But he had proven himself as an engine builder and a competitive driver, and he beat the best the Hemi enthusiasts could throw at him, and this was very satisfying.

Conway reflected on the issue many years later. "You know I took on the Hemi cars and beat them repeatedly. The Hemi boys got together and filed a protest, and NHRA reacted on their behalf. There are too many Hemi guys out there, and they were complaining very loudly; too many Hemi fans as well. We can't make all those fans, drivers, and owners angry. It would cost too much money.

Today in 2023, I could race that combination and be legal because NHRA has the Hemi boys in their own class. Now they can only beat up on each other!"

Conway returned to racing the Corvette in SS/HA until he got the new car ready. He refreshed the 454/365 engine after pulling out the LS7. He wanted to go to Columbus and dominate the class before retiring the Corvette.

April 1986, NHRA Spring Nationals, Columbus, Ohio

The car was ready in time for the spring nationals in Columbus, Ohio. He passed tech and qualified in SS/HA, and made it to the finals in his class.

His competitor was a well-to-do businessman from the Dayton area racing a big block Nova. "I changed my slicks for the next round, a decision I made due to the heat and track conditions," said Conway. "I was kneeling on one knee checking the air pressure when the Nova driver walked up to me and started talking." "I know you're faster than me, but if you let me win, I'll give you all the money I have on me" Conway was shocked. He didn't know what to do, so without looking up at the driver; he said, "How much you got?" The driver said, "Three thousand dollars." At first, Conway was tempted. "What I could do with three thousand dollars was huge," he thought. The more he thought about it, the more he realized he had never tanked a run before in his life, and he didn't want to start now. "I think I'll pass; you alright with that," Conway said. The driver walked off to his pit without a word.

The driver of the Nova was a wealthy man, and this was his home track. He was trying to buy a win in hopes of getting his first "Wally" and bragging rights with the local folks. He had failed; Conway wasn't for sale.

The two staged, the green light went on, and Conway defeated the Nova with little effort. He wins another Wally for his efforts and decides to participate in the Super Stock Top Eliminator rounds. He gets to the semi-finals and red lights against Phil Hardee. They will meet again.

As Conway continued his winning ways, so did Carla. A milestone in Carla's life was met when she graduated with an educational degree in the late spring. She was certified to teach grades 1 through 8, but the school system had very few jobs to offer when she graduated. Carla was disappointed and decided to work full-time at the bank until a teaching position that fit her needs arose. For her graduation, Conway bought Carla a new 1986 Mercury Sable.

During the summer, Conway worked on his new car, the Olds Super Stocker, with Mike Pustleny, a professional race car fabricator. This would be the first car Conway would race with a full-time sponsor, R &R Chassis, owned by Rick Fuller.

The car was ready to test in August, so Conway attended a points meet at the Bowling Green, Kentucky, drag strip. He wanted to run the car several times to get the bugs out and get a feel for it. While at the track, a friend of Conway's named Kenny was hanging out with his competitor Phil Hardee in the pits. Kenny liked anyone with a beer, and the Hardee crew supplied plenty to Kenny while trying to milk him for as much information as they could about Conway's new race car. Phil told Kenny, "Conway will never outrun me, ever!" Kenny staggered back to Conway's pit and told him what was said.

This made Conway angry, and reinforced, in part, why Conway had built the car. He was going after Phil Hardee in his Firebird; there was no love lost between the two men, with Phil bragging about his most recent win against Conway at Columbus. The showdown would occur at the US Nationals the following week.

The number of entries in the GT/FA class at the US Nationals in 1986 was huge, but Conway qualified, and eliminations began. As predicted by Conway, after four rounds, he was in the final along with Phil Hardee in his Firebird.

"The Firebird had better aerodynamics and a shorter wheelbase than the Cutlass Oldsmobile," said Conway. "Phil was running about 1/10th of a second faster than me during the eliminations, so I had my work cut out for me.

The two men stage, the light turns green, and Conway "trees" the Firebird off the line. He never looked back as he crossed the finish line for another class win at the US Nationals! He received another "Wally" for his collection; but this time, it was a revenge win; it felt good.

November 1986

Conway travels to Suffolk, Virginia, for his annual record-breaking attempt trip. The competition is stiffer this time; it's Phil Hardee again.

Conway makes a run and breaks the record, Hardee makes a run and breaks the record, Conway makes a run and breaks the record, and this goes on all afternoon until Hardee sends a message through a mutual friend to Conway, "I got no more to offer, that's it, I'm done for the day."

Conway fires up the Olds, goes to the track, and breaks his record again. "I wanted to ensure Hardee wasn't bluffing, so I made another pass. It was like beating my chest a little; I wanted to rub it in." Conway was relentless when teaching his competition a lesson if they were intentionally rude to him.

Per NHRA rules, the car is required to go to the NHRA tear-down barn to certify his record. The NHRA inspector in charge was Bob Lang, a man Conway felt was critical of him in past events.

Conway removed the valve covers, the intake/carburetor, and the heads. While doing this, Lang had his inspectors check every inch of his car, the dates on the seatbelts, traction bar height, and everything they could think of. The other cars were breezing through the inspection; most were in and out, but not Conway's car. He was still there with multiple inspectors using a fine toothed comb on the Olds. The car passed tech, and now the inspectors were checking the engine. They checked the bore and stroke, deck height, and the tops of the pistons for gas ports; they inspected the carburetor.

In the Super Stock class, the ports in the heads had to be stock in appearance, and the combustion chambers had to measure stock in cubic centimeters. The heads checked out regarding cubic centimeters, but Lang wanted more.

"He took one of the heads and inspected the intake ports. The entire time he inspects it, he shakes his head," said Conway. After about a half hour, he said, "Come here, Witten! These heads don't look right. Are you going to tell me the intake port is legal?" Conway was just a few inches from the inspector, both staring at each other eye to eye. "Why do you have a problem with the head Lang," said Conway. "It just doesn't look right to me," Lang said. After his US Nationals class win, Conway directed his attention to the seals still on the engine from the NHRA Tech inspection.

"Look, my engine hasn't been apart since the Indy inspection; they passed the engine and saw no issue with the heads!" Lang paused briefly and said, "Get a new pair before the next race!" He walked off, clearly disgusted.

As Conway reflects on that day, he laughs and says," Lang was showing me his superiority, his attitude was hardly professional. He always gave me a hard time; I guess he didn't like me."

We contacted Bob Lang at his office; he is still with the NHRA. Bob told us that he remembered Conway as "A nice person." He chose not to respond to other questions.

CHAPTER 5
ASSASSIN STRIKES AGAIN
1987-1991

In 1987 Conway retired the Corvette, leaving the Olds as his only race car. But the winning continued.

August 1987

Conway entered the 5th annual Lucas Oil Nationals at the drag strip in Brainerd, Minnesota. He goes all the way at this event and wins Top Eliminator in the Super Stock class. His post-race teardown was conducted and NHRA officials found no issues, despite having the same heads that were used in Virginia. His payday was $12,000.

Carla was winning too. She was enjoying the banking business and decided to make it her career. With her personality and education, she was going places. It was only a short time until she was promoted.

When it came to the couple's religious experience, Conway and Carla attend church on occasion, usually just on holidays.

But, in 1987, Conway felt inspired to participate in a 'Racers for Christ" service, which was held on Sunday mornings at all the significant NHRA events. "I'm not sure what came over me; I just decided to attend one morning," said Conway. "I saw Eddie Hill at my first service and was impressed." Eddie, owner of 12 national titles in top fuel dragsters and drag boats, was a devout Christian writing articles about drag racing for the Christina Motorsports Magazine. From that day forward, Conway attended Sunday morning services at the drag strip whenever he was there.

1988

During the summer of 1988, Conway was provided another opportunity that many drag races never get. To explain, we must travel back in time and visit with Jim DeFrank.

Jim grew up in Pittsburg, PA, and was a car guy early in life. He loved fast cars, drag strips, and custom car shows. In 1965 Jim packed up his belongings in a 1955 Chevy and headed west to California with his new wife Loraine.

His goal was to be a businessman in the auto parts industry, and he slowly worked his way up from a laborer at 20th Century Fox Studios, then becoming a Snap-on Tool Salesman. From there it was a natural move to become an auto parts store owner, moving on to being co-owner in a mail order auto parts company, and finally the owner of his own company, California Car Cover and the original California Duster. His pastime was drag racing.

In 1986 he brought his two Super Stock Hemi cars to the NHRA Motor Craft Nationals in Gainesville, Florida, to compete in SS/AA and SS/BA classes. The SS/BA car was a '64 Dodge lightweight, the SS/AA car was a Barracuda, in the nation's top five fastest Hemi cars.

"I first heard of Conway Witten after he beat all the Hemi cars at the '85 US Nationals. I thought, let's see if he can outrun my Hemi cars," said Jim. "Well, it didn't take long, Conway put both my cars on the trailer, and I was just as humble as possible. I was curious about this kid and started asking about his history, and I discovered he was an engine builder for Mike Keown in Louisville, Kentucky."

Not long after that, Jim was ready to switch drag racing classes. He sold the Hemi cars and bought two 1988 Camaros. "I called a friend in the Louisville area inquiring about building some racing transmissions for me," said Jim. "The discussion soon changed to Conway Witten.

"My friend had spent an entire day with Conway and his team at a local drag strip testing new parts. He told me he had never seen anyone more thorough, quality oriented, precise, and professional than Conway. Test after test, they were looking for the absolute best combination.

He was in and out the car, leading his team, twisting wrenches, and taking notes. It was indeed a learning experience for my friend, and I was convinced Conway was the man for one of my cars."

In the summer of 1988, Jim flew out to Louisville and personally asked Conway to drive one of the Camaros in competition.

"Conway asked only one question after I gave him the details," said Jim. He said, "May I build the engine for the car?" asked Conway.

"Uh, I was going to suggest that, Conway," laughed Jim.

Right before work began on the DeFrank Camaro; Conway took the Olds to the US Nationals in Indy and won his class. He sold the Oldsmobile, and by request, took a friend's Camaro, (one he had built the engine for) and won his class at Montreal.

A little later that year, Conway drove to Gulfport, Mississippi, to pick up the DeFrank Camaro. Jim had contracted a shop there to build the chassis. Once back home, Conway assembled the front suspension, built the engine for SS/GTBA, and finished setting up the car. The car was painted, and testing was done at a local track.

Conway and the crew at Mike Keown's shop also built the engine for the DeFrank Super Stock Camaro that was going to race on the west coast in SS/GTAA. DeFrank said, "I looked like the perfect example of "If I can't beat 'em, I'll join them!"

DeFrank would sponsor the Camaro with little if any, out-of-pocket expenses for Conway during 1989 and 1990.

"Conway was just awesome behind the wheel and under the hood of my Camaro," said Jim. "He was unbeaten in class racing for two seasons, set national records, and won the US Nationals."

Jim went on to tell a story about Conway that touches his heart to this day. "I have a son, Jim Jr. He was between 9 and 11 when Conway was racing our car. We would fly out for the national events and see Conway race as much as possible. I would go to the garage and hang out at times, too, to be around Conway.

"Conway spent quality time with Jim Jr. He showed him everything there was to know about the race car, told him about building engines, and shared all kinds of racing stories with Jimmy too."

Conway still maintains a relationship with Jimmy Jr, who fondly recalls his relationship with Conway and their time together as a kid.

"Conway was very focused and intense back in those days, although he was busy racing, and working two jobs, he always took time to talk to me. I was just a kid, but it meant so much for Conway to spend time with me, answering my questions and showing me all the different things it took to build a great race car." Jim Jr. went on to say to said he used many things Conway taught him during his racing career. "Conway left a large detailed notebook in the Camaro for us when the car was returned after two years of racing. I used that notebook repeatedly when I started racing the same car five years later."

When Jim Jr. turned 16 in 1995, he started drag racing the 1988 Camaro, upon the promise to his father to keep his grades up. Jim Jr. did just that, and he started racing in the Super Stock division, where today he has an impressive resume of racing achievements: 16-time Division 7 Champion, 5-time NHRA Super Stock National Champion, 19 NHRA National Events wins, 52 NHRA Divisional Event wins, 2-time NHRA National Event Double-Up Winner, 2010 US Nationals Indy winner in Super Stock.

Conway raced the Camaro in late 1988 with tremendous success. In 1989 he continued to win as he traveled the Midwest, east, and Southern US.

It was a great racing season, and he was undefeated in his class in time for the US Nationals.

In late 1988 Conway met Gale Powley, an Erie, Pennsylvania businessman contracted at the time by Mike Keown to build the shop a dynamometer. Over the next few months, Gale realized Conway had proficient engine-building skills and taught him a great detail about cylinder head porting. Gale was also a self-taught racer and engine builder since the late 1960s, and didn't share his knowledge with just anyone. A few years later, Gale's friendship would bring Conway an excellent opportunity.

September 4, 1989, US Nationals, Indianapolis, Indiana

Once again, round by round, Conway took on the competition in the DeFrank Camaro, making it to the final round with Jim DeFrank looking on. Conway's last competitor that year was the one and only Jim Boudreau from Tewksbury, MA. Jim was 48 years old and had been racing since 1964 with a remarkable resume. He was racing a late-model Camaro IROC similar to Conway's with all the latest Lingenfelter go-fast parts. Conway had his hands full with this guy, and he knew it.

The two drivers staged, the Christmas tree turned green, and both Camaros were off with their front wheels off the ground. The race was close, but Conway crossed the finish line first, another NHRA US Nationals class win. "I was jumping up and down yelling at the top of my lungs, we won Indy, we won Indy," said Jim. I was very proud of Conway and his team; what a great job against a competitor like Boudreau."

"Yes, I remember that race," said now 82-year-old Jim Boudreau from his home in Tewksbury. "Conway took the win, and I returned to the pits talking to myself." Jim went on to say that there were three competitors in that era that he would rather not face, especially in a final round: Butch Williams, Dick Butler, and of course, Conway Witten. Jim is still racing a B/S 1969 Camaro and works six hours daily at his automotive garage.

Maple Grove Raceway, Reading, Pennsylvania, October 1989

Conway showed up to try and set a national record in Super Stock GT-BA in the Camaro. He had a fierce competitor that day, a guy driving a Chevy Cavalier. Conway would make a run, break the record, go the scales and weigh, stop at the NHRA tent, and have the fuel tested. His competitor would make a run, break the record, and do the same. This went on for three passes from each car. Finally, Conway set the record again; his competitor had given up.

During the post-race teardown, the NHRA tech confronted Conway about silicone on the air cleaner stud. "Everyone plugged the hole to prevent fuel sloshing; it was no big deal," said Conway. However, the inspector was making a big deal out of it and pointed out an area on the carburetor that looked suspicious to him.

The inspector was loud and confrontational, and for the first time, Conway lost his temper to the point of doubling up his fist and approaching the inspector with the intent to harm. Thankfully Mike Keown stepped in between the two men and talked Conway out of a potentially grave mistake.

"It's not worth it, Conway," said Mike, "Calm down and walk away!" Conway moved away, and Mike took over the rest of the inspection. The suspicious area on the carburetor turned out to be factory deburring marks, and the plugged hole was a common practice, not a violation of the rules. Conway was awarded the national record, but it left a bad taste in his mouth regarding the conduct of the NHRA inspector. The following season would once again bring a confrontation with NHRA tech inspectors, but the outcome would be different.

1990

Conway once again won every race in his class during the first quarter of 1990. Jim's east coast friends were telling him that his Camaro, driven by Conway Witten, was super fast, even faster than the class above him, the SS/GTAA class. Jim was thrilled and planned to attend the Gator Nationals in March.

March 1990, NHRA Motorcraft Gator Nationals

The field was large, and Conway qualified in the top ten at Gainesville. He did his job round after round and made it to the finals. His opponent this time was Fred Atkinson from Damascus, Georgia, driving a late model Camaro. The two Camaro drivers launched at the start, with both pulling their wheels off the ground. At the big end, Conway had an ET of 9.69 compared to Fred's 9.85.

Conway took the car into the tech area for the mandatory tear-down and inspection. The engine had been given a complete overhaul after setting the national record in October, consisting of taking the engine apart, having the rods and crank checked for damage, honing the block, doing a valve job, milling the heads, and installing new rings, bearings, and valve springs.

The car had the same chassis, transmission, rear end, and other components.

During tech, the engine was deemed legal; the entire car checked out until NHRA conducted the wheelbase check.

Sitting on an unlevel surface when the first measurement was taken, the tech told Conway the car was 1/8 of an inch too short. Conway suggested they roll it to level ground and measure again. They did, and the tech once again said it was too short.

Conway and Jim DeFrank were livid; the car had been checked several times before and had passed the complete inspection. Both men realized that the inspector was asserting his authority and playing hardball. The car was disqualified, and Conway finished the weekend watching the races from the stands.

Conway and Jim discussed the inspection outcome and felt that the NHRA inspector was making an example out of him. Conway had always suspected that some of NHRA inspectors were after him for some reason; this shed some light on his beliefs.

DeFrank and Conway decided to move up in class to SS/GT-AA, and since the NHRA rules allowed it, they decided to experiment and use an engine Conway had already built using spare parts left over from his Corvette.

April 1990, NHRA Southern Nationals, Atlanta Georgia

Conway entered the Super Stock GT-AA class with the budget engine now installed. He wasn't sure the engine would hold up, so he brought a second engine just in case. During class eliminations, he destroyed the field, running at 9:40 to the competitors at 9:60. He won the class, went through the NHRA Tech inspection again, and passed. Not one word was said about the wheelbase of his car.

While in the pits after the inspection Conway was approached by a racer named Glenn from Canada, a driver that Conway had beaten that day. The man was so impressed by the performance of Conway's Camaro he demanded to buy the engine right there, then, and now. "I want that engine, and I have the cash to buy it now," said the man excitedly.

Mike Keown and Conway explained that the engine was built with spare parts, and they couldn't guarantee that it would hold up. The man was insistent. Again, Mike and Conway tried to talk him out of it.

"I won't take no for an answer; I want to take that engine home with me today," said Glenn. With that said, a price was agreed on, and the man paid cash right out of his pocket. Conway and his crew pulled the engine out and delivered it to the Canadian.

May 1990, NHRA Points Race, Indianapolis, Indiana

Conway had replaced his engine and was once again running SS/GT-BA.

He had just finished the pre-race safety inspection when someone told him Glenn was running low ETs with his old engine. Conway would only face Glenn today if both made it to Super Stock eliminations; however, he was happy for Glenn, after all, that was his engine. The following day Glenn found Conway and reported the good news. "The car is running faster than it ever has. I couldn't be happier."

Not long after, Conway saw Glenn's car being towed into the pits by a track wrecker, and soon, Glenn asked Conway and Mike to go look at the car. The hood was open when Conway and his crew arrived, and he looked the engine over. It was utterly destroyed. A rod came through the block with such force, it sheared the fuel pump mounting boss off the front of the engine. The block was history, and the car was done for the day.

Glenn, red-faced and angry, stood next to Conway, and said with disgust, "What should I do now?" Conway paused for a moment and looked at Glenn with a straight face. "Glenn, I wouldn't race that engine anymore today!"

Conway's crew broke down laughing while Glenn stood there looking dumbfounded. Conway managed to get away from there before a fight broke out.

Conway won his class and was loading up to leave the track when Glenn walked over to the pit. "Will you build me a new engine?" he asked. Conway shook his hand

and said, "Of course, Glenn, no problem." Conway and Glenn were friends from that day, doing business several times a year.

Conway went on to win his class at the 1990 US Nationals. He was ready to move up in class, so he returned the DeFrank Camaro and agreed to transport the car to Kansas City, where another driver would take it to California.

That December, Conway and Carla left for Kansas City, just a little over 500 miles from Louisville, transporting the car in an enclosed trailer. It was raining when they left, and after a couple of hours, Conway became sleepy, so Carla took over driving.

Conway got into the back seat of the crew cab truck to take a nap. When he woke up, Carla had lost control of the truck while crossing an icy bridge. The truck was fishtailing all over, and Carla was struggling to keep the truck on the road "I yelled at her to hit the trailer brake; she didn't understand. So, I reached out and hit the trailer brake switch, and that straightened out the truck and trailer," said Conway.

Carla pulled over, and Conway took over the driving duties. Both of them were shaking after the incident. They managed to deliver the car and got back home safe.

Conway had been planning a change for several months to a different class and a faster car. He made numerous calls, talked to people who raced in the class he was considering, read the NHRA rule book, and decided. "I want to race in competition eliminator. I want a dragster!"

In 1954, Mickey Thompson was the first to develop what is now known as a "slingshot" dragster, a racing chassis that placed the driver behind the rear axle and coupled the engine and transmission directly to the differential of the vehicle. Since then, designs have changed from the shorter wheelbase front engine dragster to the long wheelbase on the rear engine dragster but still using the same concept, lightweight body, massive V8 engines, equaled crazy mph and ET in the quarter mile.

Conway found a dragster chassis builder in New York and hired him to build one. Conway would build and install the engine himself, of course, but this guy built dragsters to spec, and Conway already knew all the dimensions he wanted in his car.

In late 1990 Conway and Carla drove to Buffalo, New York, to pick up the car. Once there, they loaded the car on an enclosed trailer Conway had bought just for the dragster, and took off for Louisville with Carla sitting next to Conway in the diesel pickup, shifting the gears of the five-speed transmission, something she liked to do.

They found a hotel room for the night and walked to a nearby restaurant. Once back in the room, Conway told Carla he would return in a few minutes. Even at 35, Conway was still a little kid at heart. He started the generator on the trailer and turned on the inside lights revealing his new pride and joy, the dragster chassis minus the running gear.

It was his; he had no partners, nobody to tell him where to race and where to be; he would decide that now. Carla, who seemed to have a new zeal about running this car, would have some responsibilities she had never had before; she would be part of the crew whenever she could take time off to go.

Looking outside the door to make sure he was alone, Conway climbed into the tiny cockpit with difficulty, but it was comfortable once seated. He grabbed the steering wheel with both hands and made racing engine noises while he pretended to be driving down the drag strip. Suddenly Conway remembered a long-ago conversation when a friend told him, "You'll get your ass kicked in that class, buddy." Conway thought, "Yah right, like the hemi cars did, like Phil Hardee did, no way!"

He wasn't arrogant, he was just good at what he did, and he couldn't wait to drive this one. Conway continued to make engine noises and race down the imaginary strip for quite some time.

He locked the trailer up and returned to the hotel room, ready to sleep. Carla, already in bed with the TV on, said, "What were you doing?" Conway admitted he was just looking at the car. With a little smile on his face he turned out the light.

Before any work was done on the new dragster, Conway had an appointment with Jim DeFrank. Right before the 1990 racing season ended, Conway received a call from him. "There's a racing team out here challenging me in the SS/GT-BA Camaro. I want to beat them; you want to help?" Conway's reply was yes. "Fantastic," said Jim, "Plan on being at the Winter Nationals next year; I will cover all expenses!"

In 1952 drag racing was in its early years, and throughout the United States, hot rodders of all ages were looking for a place to race legally.

A car club known as the "Choppers of Pomona," along with a police officer and his chief, petitioned the Los Angeles County Board of Supervisors to lease the parking lot at the LA County Fairgrounds to race on. The county agreed on one stipulation, the car club had to provide its insurance.

The parking area was only gravel at the time, but through fundraisers and other events, the club raised the money to have an area paved with asphalt to race on.

This would be the birth of the Pomona Drag Strip, hosting the first National Hot Rod Association's (NHRA) event, "The Southern California Championships," in April 1953.

On February 19, 1961, the first NHRA Winter Nationals, nicknamed "The Big Go West," was held at Pomona. In February of 2023, the sixty-second running of this event was held, making it the second-oldest event in drag racing history.

Pomona is perhaps the most beloved drag strip in the United States due to its history, and in 1991, at the 30th annual running of this event, Conway Witten, the Assassin, a hired gun, was there to win the SS/GT-BA class for Jim DeFrank.

February 1991, NHRA Winter Nationals, Pomona, California

In late 1990 Jim DeFrank had been challenged by several southern California drag racers to bring his SS/GTBA Camaro to the first big shootout of 1991, the winter nationals. It was a challenge in good fun, but both Jim and Conway took it seriously.

"Jim wanted me to spank this group in the SS/GT - BA class, so he flew me out to California for the event," said Conway. "I normally didn't race out west, but I wanted to do Jim a favor." One racing team, in particular, was vocal about the matchup, the team of Vince DeGani, and Dean Tait with car owner George Wejbe. Their car was a late model Oldsmobile Calais with all the modern go-fast parts. They were very competitive and good people; however, the "Assassin" from Kentucky would drive the DeFrank Camaro, a factor no one had figured on.

Round after round came and went in the Super Stock GT-BA class at Pomona with the two finalists, as predicted, Witten and Tait. They would be racing each other for the class win. They lined up, green lights on, and Conway took the win for the "Wally" in class.

Jim DeFrank hugged Conway after he passed the mandatory NHRA teardown; the Assassin strikes again!

This would be the first and last time Conway would race in California, and it remains one of the top moments in his racing career.

CHAPTER 6
A NEW CAR, NEW HOUSE, ANOTHER WALLY
1991-1993

The most popular classes in drag racing in 1991 were Top Fuel Dragsters, Top Fuel Funny Cars, Pro Stocks, and Pro Stock Motorcycles. Becoming a driver or part of a team in these classes takes tremendous skill, determination, and time. Most people that participate in the above classes do it on a full-time basis. They go to every event annually, eighteen in all in '91.

Pomona, California, twice a year
Phoenix, Arizona
Houston, Texas
Gainesville, Florida
Atlanta, Georgia
Memphis, Tennessee
Columbus, Ohio
Montreal, Canada
Englishtown, New Jersey
Denver, Colorado
Sonoma, California
Seattle, Washington
Brainerd, Minnesota
Indianapolis, Indiana
Reading, Pennsylvania,
Topeka, Kansas
Dallas, Texas

The balance of NHRA participants competed in approximately eleven other classes, including Competition Eliminator, or simply Comp. Most of these people are not full-time racers, and they travel to selected events and participate as their budget allows.

The Comp class is broken down into the following:

A through G Gas Dragster, A through F Econo Dragster, AA, AAT, BB, BBT, A through N Altered, A through D Street Roadster, A through E Econo Altered and (Gas) Funny Car, and finally A through C Super Modified.

Back home in Kentucky, Conway began to prepare the dragster to race. He chose the Competition Eliminator Class he wanted to compete in, B/ED Econo Dragster. The class is determined by total car weight, including the driver, divided by total engine displacement. The B/ED Econo Dragster class consists of cars that resemble "Top Fuel Rails," long bodies, and low chassis with a cockpit and rear engine. The engines are carbureted and use gas only; no exotic fuel mixture is allowed. These cars are capable of 7-second runs at over 180 mph in the quarter mile, at least two seconds and 40 mph faster in the quarter mile than his Corvette had ever gone. In drag racing, this is a tremendous step up in skill sets.

Conway's first dragster had a 238-inch wheelbase, a 12 bolt Chevy rear end, a small block Chevy trainer engine, a low-budget build designed to help him break into the new class, a power glide transmission (only two forward speeds) with a valve body brake, skinny bike cycle type tires on the front and huge racing slicks on the rear. It weighed only 1,340 pounds compared to a modern compact car that weighs 2,600 to 3 000 pounds. The dragster had a parachute to slow it down at the end of a run, the first time he had ever used one.

Conway had to get a special license to compete in the new car, much like he did with the first dragster he raced 15 years earlier. He drove to Ohio Valley Raceway, just ten miles from his home, and completed the requirements without issues. He wanted to be competitive but also take it easy for the first few runs and get used to it. Conway had done his homework and already knew who the fastest person in his division was Doug Stewart, who was running 7. 60's at the time.

Conway realized the cost of racing the dragster in the venues he wanted to participate in would require a larger budget. In recent weeks he had been talking to Memphis, Tennessee native Gordon Holloway, who had expressed interest in joining Conway's racing team. They had known each other for ten years because Gordon was a sales manager for a Camshaft company and had clients in all the major automotive sports.

After a few meetings it was agreed Gordon would invest in the operation and attend as many events as he could as a working team member. "I watched Conway grow up in the sport and thought he was an up and coming star," said Gordon.

"My first race was at Indy during points meet. I didn't do very well, but I was still learning the car and the setup," said Conway. "I didn't like the carburetor I was using, so I sent a used one to Gary Williams, a nationally known carburetor builder and asked him to set it up for me; his motto was "Trust Me.""

At the next race in Bowling Green, Kentucky, he went 7.70 during a qualifying session right off the trailer, which was not good enough to compete with his competition.

Gordon suggested they replace the carburetor with the rebuilt one Gary Williams had sent back. "We replaced the carburetor, and I ran a 7.48," said Conway. "Gordon handed me a t-shirt that Gary Williams had sent along with the rebuilt carburetor; it said "Trust Me" on the front of the shirt!"

Conway made it to the semi-finals that day in only his second time out, but a red light put him on the trailer.

For the next race in Columbus, the team decided to replace the training engine with a 340 cubic inch Chevy engine they affectionately nicknamed "John Wayne." "Everyone asked me why I called that engine John Wayne," said Conway. "It had 800 horses, but at idle, it was smooth and quiet; in competition, it was like a wild animal; it came alive the second you gave it the gas. It reminded me of John Wayne in McLintock," said Conway. "I won't; I won't, the hell I won't."

(Conway refers to John Wayne's line in the movie, McLintock, when he tries hard to hold his temper and finally loses it by slugging a guy.)

NHRA Spring Nationals, Columbus, Ohio, May 199

Conway and his team arrive in Columbus with the new engine installed on the dragster. The first qualifying run was a 7.27 at 185 mph, which was fast enough to qualify, but Conway wanted to see just how fast this new engine would take him.

The next run starts off just as quickly, but the car starts to mishandle at mid-track; bucking, wobbling, and starting to fishtail. Conway backs off and gets the car straightened up and under control.

It was a scary ride for Conway and at the shutdown area he was agitated. Gordon and Chuck ask him what happened and Conway snapped at them, "Just get me back to the pits." Conway was acting strangely; he kept his distance and stayed in the car while his team towed him back to their pit area. He normally let Chuck steer the dragster while Gordon towed with the crew cab, Conway would always review his time slips, but not this time.

Back at the pits, Conway grabs his overnight bag out of the truck and disappears. About 30 minutes later, he returns, ready to make another pass. Both Gordon and Chuck were curious, "Where did you run off to, buddy" said Gordon. "Well, if you have to know all the details I had to change my shorts!" yelled Conway.

Although Conway was not a partying type of guy, some of his friends were. An example of this always brings tears of laughter to Conway's eyes.

1991 Indy Points Race

Someone stole the "Reece" trailer hitch from Mike Farrell's truck, Conway's boss at the trucking company and a fellow racer. Conway told him he had one at home, so Mike leaves immediately to get it, not saying a word to his crew members, and makes the 90 minute drive to Louisville. He picks up the hitch but decides to spend the night at home and return early the following morning.

Conway goes to bed, but Mike's crew starts partying and they all become very inebriated. After a while they started looking for Mike, he's nowhere to be found. The party went on, the drinking continued until the wee hours of the morning, until finally all have passed out except for one crew member. Still very drunk, and still unable to find Mike, the crew member calls the police to file a missing person report. While in the middle of describing Mike over the phone, Mike walks into the hotel room and the guy on the telephone freaks out. In a drunken stupor, the guy goes, "Where the hell you been? We thought you were missing?"

By then everyone is up and listening to the conversation. Mike is standing there in disbelief, "Hang up the phone dude, I went to Louisville last night." Everyone starts yelling, "Mike's back, Mike's back, while laughter filled the room.

July 1991, Martin Michigan, NHRA Popular Hot Rodding Nationals

In only his fourth outing with the new dragster, Conway made it to the finals and won the event, beating the more experienced Brain Stufflebeam, a truly remarkable feat.

The new car brought Conway and Carla a little closer as a couple, and they were enjoying their time together at the drag strip. When Conway was running super stock, Carla didn't have much to do. Now, when she was able to attend meets, she had a role on the team that included packing the parachute after each run, towing the dragster with their truck from the shut down area to the pit, and guiding Conway into the water box and the traction zone when he completed his burnout. Carla also kept the trailer stocked with supplies.

The weekend before the Beech Bend point race, Conway, Gordon, and Mike Keown took the dragster's engine to Larry Clark's Speed Shop in Knoxville, Tennessee.

Larry had a Dyno, and Conway had rented it for a day to tune up his engine. Larry, a practicing attorney for several years, quit the profession to do what he loved best, building racing motors. He was well-known in motor racing and built engines for several pro stocks and NASCAR teams.

While on the Dyno, the team members tried to find more horsepower but Conway added too much air to the air /fuel mixture, which burned up a piston and caused damage to a head. Aggravated and tired, the men loaded up the engine and headed home, knowing many hours of repair work were in front of them.

While driving back to Louisville their bad luck continued. Conway was suddenly stricken with pain in his side; it was intense and continued for several minutes. Finally, he couldn't stand it any longer and pulled up to a hospital. He went into to the ER and explained that he was in pain and needed meds. He couldn't stand up straight, and the pain was so intense he was in tears.

It was evident the attending nurse was suspicious. Mike Keown had gone in with Conway and was standing nearby.

Conway was asked to lie on a small bed in a small treatment room. Mike realized that the nurse thought Conway might be a junkie seeking painkillers and he yelled at her, "Listen, lady, my friend doesn't drink, smoke, or take drugs, he works for me, and he's in pain; PLEASE, GIVE HIM SOMETHING!"

With that, the nurse disappeared, and five minutes later, she returned and gave Conway a shot for the pain. The doctor examined him, did some blood work, and informed him that his pain was due to a kidney stone. Conway passed the stone a couple of hours later, was given a prescription, and returned to Louisville. He went to bed that night and slept hard; the following week would be rough.

Still working two jobs, on Monday morning, Conway disassembled the engine at the engine shop and identified the actual damage. He worked that evening at the trucking company and returned to the shop early to work on the car. This went on for the rest of the week; Conway took only one short nap between Monday morning and Friday night. He managed to repair the engine, reassemble it, reinstall it in the car, and leave for Beach Bend Friday morning.

The hard work paid off; Conway won the points meet in his class after going many rounds against a large field of cars. Beech Bend is always held the weekend before the US Nationals, and the competition is always fierce.

Conway took his wife and crew out to celebrate the win for a seafood dinner. Carla and Gordon decided to have crab legs, and according to Conway, they had a contest to see who could eat the most in one sitting.

"I couldn't believe the number of crab legs they ate," said Conway, "Their plates were overflowing with crab shells, spilling on the table and the floor at one point!"

Labor Day Weekend, 1991, NHRA US Nationals, Indianapolis, Indiana

The best of the best come to the nationals every year to test their skills against competition from all over the US and Canada. Conway Witten was present with his new car and the recent win at Beach Bend the weekend before.

He qualified fourth in a field of twelve cars and was again in the zone, winning race after race. Conway faced the legend David Nickens from Conroe, Texas, in the semi-finals.

Nickens was the winningest driver in the competition eliminator at that time and was difficult to beat. Conway drove into the water box and did his burnout, both drivers staged, and at the green, they took off.

Conway knew something was wrong within a split second. He didn't have enough power, and Nickens crossed the finish line for the win. Later Conway would learn he broke a valve spring while doing his burnout, which caused his engine to lose power and the race. Nickens went on to win the class and took home the Wally.

October 3, 1991,
Door Slammer Nationals, Ohio Valley Drag Strip, Louisville, Kentucky

Conway is back on his home track, trying to qualify for the event. It's his 36th birthday, and he always felt lucky on his birthday while racing.

He makes a good pass, and at the finish line, his parachute is deployed and tangles in the wheelie bars. The car goes out of control and slams into a guard rail, causing a large piece of debris to fly off the rail, coming within inches of the cockpit. The car's aluminum body and chrome molly chassis are totaled. Conway's opponent crashes his car, too, while avoiding the debris created by Conway's crash. That car is also totaled, but the driver was alright. Carla drives the tow truck to the scene with tears in her eyes and is relieved when she sees Conway out of the car. He is unhurt and is already trying to figure out the cause. This is accident number three; one more is coming. Racing for Conway was over for 1991.

"Conway's reputation and accomplishments in competition eliminator were on a distinct uphill climb after his US Nationals appearance in September," said friend Bob Toy. "The accident was a setback, but Conway sure had the old guard in the class turning their heads."

"Conway was a determined, smart racer," said Gerry Merrick, a fellow racer and friend of Conway's. "I raced in the same class with Conway and could never beat him. Our cars were almost identical because the same person built them almost simultaneously. The dragsters were complex cars to drive. If they went straight, you had no problems; if they didn't, get out of the throttle because they would get out of control quickly.

I nicknamed my dragster "Evil," I always thought I was on edge or out of control with it. I never wrecked mine, but I came close too many times.

"I sold my car in 1995, and the buyer wrecked on his third race, barrel rolling and totaling the car. He was knocked out but survived; he was fortunate."

In late October, Carla and Conway took their first trip together that was not racing-related. Carla wanted to see the southwest, so they flew to Albuquerque, New Mexico and rented a car, and then drove in a big loop through Northwestern New Mexico, southwestern Colorado, and parts of Arizona. They rode the Durango Silverton steam engine and ate authentic Mexican food. They visited the Grand Canyon, the Sonora Desert National Monument, and Tombstone, Arizona. They got to see wild horses, Boot Hill, and other attractions. They were gone for ten days, and Carla hoped this would be the start of more personal time together.

During the off season Conway and Carla would snuggle in bed on Saturday mornings in the late fall and winter and watch their favorite cartoon show, Ren and Stimpy. The character Ren Höek was a short-tempered Chihuahua Dog, and Stimpson J. "Stimpy" Cat was a dimwitted happy-go-lucky cat. The couple enjoyed the show so much that they gave each other nicknames; Conway became Ren, and Carla became Stimpy, each signing cards and notes using their new names.

1992-1993

After returning from vacation, Conway took what was left of the dragster back to the builder in New York State. He wanted the car rebuilt to his standards this time, which included a few changes.

First, he wanted the car five inches longer, making it 243 inches, just a shade over twenty feet.

Second, he wanted a carbon fiber adjustable wing installed on the nose of the car.

The third modification was the installation of slip joints, a device that allowed the car to flex while going down the track. The slip joints are installed on the frame's top rail, with two tubes fitting inside one another. All three modifications would improve handling, which equated to a faster and safer car.

Driving the dragster takes a different skill level than driving a door slammer car, a conventional car with doors, and hood. Control is the main factor in handling a car that weighs only 1,300 pounds with 800 horsepower. For comparison, the average daily driver weighs 3.500 pounds in the US, with horsepower rated at 200.

Conway's car was completed at the end of November 1991. For Conway, the 1992 season would start in March.

In 1992 Conway and Carla bought a property in Jeffersonville, Indiana, just a mile across the Ohio River Bridge from Louisville. They designed a home and hired contractors to build it. Carla managed most of the home details while Conway continued working two jobs at the engine shop and the trucking company. Carla had just received one of many promotions she would later receive at the bank she worked at in Louisville. She was now a project manager for a bank that had branches throughout the United States

Conway raced the new dragster at a few points meets in early 1992, winning his share of races. The car seemed much more stable with his incorporated changes, and he was feeling better about the handling.

April 1992 - 22nd Annual NHRA Le Grand National
Molson Sanair International drag strip, Montreal, Canada

Conway traveled to Montreal to test his skills at the international level. Carla made the trip too, and her knowledge of the French language, learned during her summer abroad with her post high school French class, she helped translate when necessary.

Conway qualified second in a large field of cars, but a red light in the second round eliminated him.

Later in the year, Conway's friend and part-time team member Gordon Holloway had an ongoing relationship with several NASCAR teams in the south through his work at a camshaft company.

He contacted Conway with some important news, three teams wanted to see Conway's head work up close and personal. Over the past few months, Gordon had bragged about Conway's skills as a head porter, and the NASCAR teams were listening.

Conway grabbed a set of his racing heads and traveled to North Carolina with Gordon to the racing shops of Rick Hendricks at Hendricks Motor Sports, Richard Childress, at Childress Racing, and Billy Hagan, at Hagan Racing Enterprises. Each group welcomed Conway to their shops, and an information exchange was conducted each time. The trip was very informative for all involved, and Conway had a great time meeting the owners, mechanics, and even some drivers.

August 1992, Beech Bend Raceway, Bowling Green, Kentucky, Points Meet

Conway qualified third at Beech Bend and was winning round after round. Four cars were left when Conway came to the line for the semi-finals, and he staged and left on the green. At mid-track, he knew he had won the race, but something didn't sound right from the engine after shutting down. Carla and the team came to the end of the track to pull the car back to the pits.

Once in the pits, they check the "John Wayne" engine and find it has dropped a valve; no more racing for Conway; he can't make the call for the final. There was one shining moment before the motor blew. Conway had set another national record in his class!

Still, it was disappointing, his primary engine was blown up, his spare needed to be better to compete at the national level, he was super busy at both jobs, and the US Nationals were only one week away. This would be the first time he would miss the nationals in ten years.

The following month Conway had an idea. Ohio Valley was holding an International Hot Rod Association meet, and they recognized a dragster class called G/ED.

The racers could use a super stock engine with any carburetor in their dragster body. He researched the field and found out the top cars were running 5.20 in the 1/8 mile. Conway had a friend that was always up for anything, Paul, agreed to loan him an engine that fit the class.

With a borrowed engine, borrowed headers, and a borrowed converter, Conway took the dragster to Ohio Valley.

When the smoke had cleared, Conway had not only won the class but also set a new national record for his class in the 1/8 mile, a 4.95.

By the end 1992, their 2,800 square feet, four bedroom, three bathroom, three car garage house was completed, and they moved into their new home on New Year's Day, 1993.

CHAPTER 7
TRAGEDY
1993

The racing year started great, with Conway winning several events. By midseason, he was third in his division and fifth in the nation in his class. After a series of transmission issues were corrected, the old faithful "John Wayne" engine was worn out. Conway had been racing it for three seasons, and the wear and tear had finally caught up with it.

By late August, Conway had a new engine built and was ready for the US Nationals. He worked until the wee hours of the morning for three days to get ready for Indy. Finally, at 4 am on the day he was to leave, after a quick run on the dyno, the engine was installed. The test showed good power but as far as track testing, he needed more time. The new engine would just have to come through for him during the qualifying run. He loaded up the "John Wayne" engine just in case.

Labor Day Weekend, 1993, NHRA US Nationals, Indianapolis, Indian

A very tired Conway, along with teammate Chuck, took the dragster to the tech line for inspection. After passing the inspection he made the first qualifying run, which was an utter disappointment. The power level was so bad he decided to change engines.

In a typical central Indiana thunderstorm, Conway and Chuck swapped engines in the dragster. They had a shelter, but the wind was blowing and the rain was coming in sideways, soaking both men before their task was over. In Conway's twenty years as a drag racer, he had faced weather like this before, and getting soaked during repairs was nothing new.

The rain delay gave the men time to finish their work. With the old reliable "John Wayne" engine back in and the track dry, Conway qualified for competition. He was now excited about his chances of winning another Wally at the US Nationals.

Every driver will tell you that "cutting a good light" is half the battle in a drag race. Good reaction times win races. Since 1982, after buying a full-size tree, Conway practiced until he could turn his back and watch the reflection through a mirror while still making a good start. Overall he was way above average when it came to cutting the lights, but not today.

After all the work, frustration, time, weather delays, and aggravation, Conway red lighted in the first round. He loaded the dragster on the trailer and headed home, without a complaint, because that's racing.

For several years Conway had considered traveling to Kansas in the early fall to race at the Topeka track. After Indy, he decided this was the year to go. He had never been there, and it was time for a change. He sat down and talked it out with Carla; she was somewhat unhappy about his decision because she couldn't go. Carla was into crafting and made small crafts in her spare time in the winter to sell at craft shows held in the summer and fall. The Saint James Art Fair held in October at Louisville was special to her and her aunt.

Conway notified Chuck and Gordon, and both could go to Topeka; so the trip was on. Conway had a month to prepare for the 580-mile trip, and he began by closely inspecting the entire car. A few minor changes were made here and there, as well as a close inspection of the valve springs and adjusting the valves. Conway had decided to use the old reliable John Wayne engine again.

One day at the engine shop, a week before Conway's trip, Gale Powley approached him. While using Mike's shop, Gale was temporarily in the area again doing engine work for a client. He asked Conway to meet with him in private during their lunch hour. "I told Conway that a wealthy local businessman had contacted me to build several Pro Stock engines for his son's new car for the 1994 racing season, and I wanted Conway to help me with this project. I was sure it would become a full-time position on a new Pro Stock team for both of us, "said Gale. That meant visiting 18 locations starting in February and lasting until November.

Racing teams typically took some time off for the holidays, but were back at it testing until the winter nationals in California in February, starting another new season. This meant time away from home, hotels, fast food, and endless hours of testing, qualifying, and racing, all with a brand-new team and owner. It was risky for a man that worked two good jobs, only traveling when he wanted to and being his own boss when it came to racing. "I wanted to think about it," said Conway. "I might have helped him build the starter motors, but I wasn't sure about the rest."

Another offer would be coming from friend Bob Toy. Bob was ready to sell his race car and invest as a full-time partner in Conway and the Dragster. He thought Conway could dominate the class with a little more budget money, as well travel the circuit full-time, racing at all 18 events. He was preparing to discuss this venture with Conway in full detail at the NHRA Fall Nationals in Ennis, Texas. He approached Conway about attending the event and Conway had tentatively agreed. "I thought Conway was just the best," said Bob. "I couldn't go to Topeka, but I wished him good luck and went home to plan my meeting with him in Texas. I was going to be organized with a written plan, a budget, the whole works."

The night before Conway left for Topeka he called his mom and dad to say hello and get caught up on what had been happening at their house. His father told him that his retirement was official but his mother would continue working. Conway told them about his trip. The elder Wittens were not race fans, they attended very few of Conway's events, but they both wished him well before hanging up. Carla and Conway had an early dinner and went to bed. It was a long trip that would take all day; at least it was interstate driving the entire way.

September 30, 1993, Louisville, Kentucky

Conway woke early, had breakfast, said goodbye to Carla, picked up Chuck, and drove to the shop. The 1986 Ford F-350 Crew Cab Dually that Conway used for towing, was connected to the to the 36-foot Chaparral 5th wheel trailer carrying the dragster, tools, and spare parts. They hit Interstate 64 heading west and drove to St. Louis, where they met Gordon, who had driven up from Memphis and parked at a friend's business. They picked up Interstate 70 and drove west to Topeka. The entire drive took a little over ten hours, and after arriving at their hotel, the men had dinner and went to bed. The racing event was scheduled for three days.

Topeka, Kansas – October 3 1993, NHRA Sears Craftsman Nationals

"Oh my God, he's not breathing, we have to get him out of the car," yelled Dan Brickey, the lead NHRA EMT.

Conway was trapped in the tiny cockpit of the dragster, unconscious and not breathing. After multiple rolls, the cage is still in place but the dragster lies on its side. The rescue team uses the HURST Jaws of Life to get Conway out of the car. There is no fire, but fuel is leaking, and the NHRA rescue teams are in full response.

While the crews are feverously working on getting Conway out of the totaled dragster, a strange unusual feeling comes over Conway, a feeling he had never felt before.

"I found myself in a place where you talk without a mouth, hear without ears, and see without eyes. It was a totally spiritual place; it was so calming. I felt like it was the most comforting place I had ever been. Time doesn't exist. A voice was there. I started to ask the voice questions in my typical cynical way.

"Where am I?"

The voice said, "You are with the Father." The language wasn't English, but I understood every word.

I then asked the voice, "Where am I going?"

The voice said, "To Heaven."

I said, "I've been so bad in this life."

The voice said, "I came to earth as Jesus Christ; anyone that believes in me will go to Heaven and be with me."

I felt the voice knew that I believed in Jesus Christ, and I said, "All right." I then asked the voice, "Which religion is the right religion?"

The voice said, "There is no right or wrong religion as long as it teaches about Jesus Christ."

I got the impression that the voice liked arguing about religion.

The voice said, "How can anyone say that a person like Billy Graham or Mother Theresa is bad?"

As the EMTs and other workers extract Conway from the dragster, the movement clears his airway. The violent snap and roll energy had caused him to regurgitate, and the debris had blocked his airway. They carefully placed his body on a backboard, put a cervical collar around his neck, and hooked him up to oxygen.

They loaded him in an ambulance and rushed him to the medical tent where a doctor was standing by. The life flight helicopter had already been called and was just seconds away from landing.

The doctor at the medical tent examined Conway and, due to his erratic breathing, decided to perform endotracheal intubation, a process where the healthcare provider inserts a tube through a person's mouth or nose, then down into their trachea (airway/windpipe). The tube keeps the trachea open so that air can get through, and the tube can connect to a machine that delivers air or oxygen. The procedure was complicated because Conway, while still totally unconscious, became combative; his arms and legs swinging wildly, and it took several medical people to hold him down physically. According to specialists,' aggressive behavior after a head injury is often the result of damage to the areas of the brain responsible for emotion and behavior, such as the frontal lobe.

Conway was loaded on a medical helicopter and transported to the nearest hospital.

The following was taken from the first Doctor's report written about his condition:

"This patient is a 38- year -old white male drag racer involved in a high-speed multiple rollover accident while driving his dragster at Heartland Park this afternoon. The patient was stated to be in respiratory arrest at the scene. During the rollovers, the patient regurgitated into the helmet, and inhaled some debris.

His airway blocked for a while, and while they were extricating him from the car, the motion from that task cleared the airway enough for him to breathe again. The NHRA doctor at the location intubated the patient apparently with a great deal of difficulty. The patient was transported here from the scene by LifeStar. On arrival here, the patient was found to have an endotracheal tube in the posterior pharynx. There were copious amounts of blood in the pharynx, and the patient was eventually, after much difficulty, reintubated.

He was pretty combative on arrival. He required multiple doses of Valium over an hour and a dose of Anectine (a muscle-relaxing agent) and Norcuron(a skeletal muscle-relaxing agent) to intubate him. He is now on a ventilator, and a nasogastric tube was also placed in service.

(The nasogastric tube is inserted through the nose, down the throat and esophagus, and into the stomach. It delivers drugs, liquids, and liquid food or it can remove substances from the stomach)

Conway was placed in the ICU while still unconscious in "critical- condition" with an uncertain outlook.

"I was in shock after the crash," said Chuck. "I ran down the track to see what I could do, but a track worker stopped me from getting too close for my safety. I could see the rescue crew using the Jaws of Life to get Conway out of there."

"I was so scared for Conway," said Gordon. "How anyone could live through what I saw happen at that track is incredible."

Once Conway was transported to the medical tent, his crew members exited the facility and waited. They saw the helicopter land and shortly after were told where the helicopter was going. Both men feared for Conway's life.

Arriving at the hospital, both Chuck and Gordon placed a phone call to Carla to break the bad news.

The beginning of the call was awkward for both men because an ICU Nurse was with them to get some information. "Hello, Carla?" Gordon said when she answered the phone. "Hello, Gordon.

Did Conway win?' asked Carla. "Uh, no, uh, Carla, Conway got hurt in an accident and a Nurse needs to know if he's allergic to anything, here she is." With that, Gordon handed the phone to the nurse, and she explained what had happened.

The earliest flight to Kansas was the following morning, so Carla packed a bag and called the intensive care Nurse's desk every hour on the hour the entire night. She didn't sleep a wink and drove to the airport to board the flight to Kansas. She arrived at the hospital late that morning.

The attending physician met Carla and gave her the grave news. "Your husband's brain has been injured. It's swelling, and there is bleeding. Although he was wearing a helmet and was strapped in, the multiple high-speed rollovers caused his head to be repeatedly struck against the roll bar on both sides of the skull. We are giving him meds for the swelling. If the swelling continues, we can do surgery but only if necessary. His chances of survival are debatable. The next 24 to 48 hours will give us much more information.

"If my husband pulls through, what should I expect?" said Carla. "That's an unknown Mrs. Witten," said the doctor.

The news was like a lead weight on Carla's chest; she was shocked, emotional, and frightened. It would take several more hours to know if Conway would even survive, let alone have permanent damage to the brain. Carla took a deep breath and went to the nearest phone. She called Conway's parents, her employer, Conway's employer, and a few other family members and friends.

Chuck and Gordon were at her side the entire time.

Representatives from the race track made arrangements for her to stay at a hotel and made available coupons for food. She could only enter Conway's room for 10 minutes every hour. It was like ten years, the stress and anxiety would be constant for the next few hours and she had to make the best of it. She couldn't think straight at first.

Carla was a woman who was always calm and professional at all times. Now she was desperately clinging to hope that her husband would even live. She would ruminate, "He's got to make it through. Oh God, please don't let him die!" She broke down, unable to control her emotions.

The epicenter of the human body is the brain. On average, weighing in at three pounds, it floats in spinal fluid and is protected by the skull. In many ways, the brain is a mystery to doctors and scientists, but all will agree that the brain is fragile.

The Mayo Clinic explains that TBI is a traumatic injury to the brain that "usually results from a violent blow or jolt to the head or body." In Conway's case, there were numerous blows to the head, potentially 30 or more, during the dramatic barrel rolling he experienced. Even with an approved racing helmet and padding on the roll cage, it just wasn't enough to prevent the injury due to the violent nature and energy of the crash.

During his accident, Conway received around thirty blows to the head, causing bruising, bleeding, and tearing of nerve fibers. Because the skull cannot expand, the brain tissue swells and the pressure inside the skull rises. This is known as increased intracranial pressure, or ICP, which can prevent blood from flowing to the brain and can cause permanent damage to brain functions. Doctors use hypertonic saline to control intracranial pressure. It works by drawing the extra water out of the brain cells into the blood vessels and allowing the kidneys to filter it out of the blood. Surgery can also be used to control swelling as a last resort. A portion of the skull is removed during a decompressive craniectomy.

Many people reached out to help; the compassion and generosity were incredible. Bob Toy, who had hoped to start a business venture with Conway, was an example.

"The following few days were like a whirlwind after Conway's accident. First, we were praying that he would live. Second, the enormous financial consequences of the event, both due to the medical costs and loss of income, would be incredible. I know in my heart that God spoke to me to do what I could do. I opened an account at my local bank and entitled it 'The Conway Witten Benevolent Fund' and set about doing whatever I could to raise money to help my friend. This included an ad in the weekly newspaper "National Dragster" printed by the NHRA. I called dozens of racers nationwide, asking them to contribute whatever they could afford to this cause."

After 48 hours of treatment, doctors met with Carla and told her the chances were good for Conway to survive. The brain swelling had stopped; however, they were not optimistic about his total recovery, which would be the next hurdle to cross.

Numerous horror stories exist regarding brain injury survivors, what they can no longer do, what has to be done for them, and so on. Carla was facing this issue. What will she see once Conway is awake? Carla would just have to wait and see.

Take the strange case of Ed Allison, a 19- year-old at the time of his accident. In 1967 Ed built a front-engine junior fuel dragster with his friend Fred Crow to compete in drag racing events in California.

While at Carlsbad Raceway making a run, the u-joint between the clutch can and rear-end broke. The clutch to exploded, sending the engine mount into the steering arm. Unable to steer, the car slammed into the guard rail, started to roll, and then shattered into pieces. The roll bar bent during the crash and Allison received severe head injuries. He had a wife and an infant son, and would spend the rest of his life in a coma, for the next 23 years, dying on May 30, 1990.

During the first ten days, Conway was in the ICU, so visitations were limited. His father, Bill, and Conway's friend Tony Clark traveled from Louisville to the hospital. Both men were in shock as they looked in on Conway and saw all the tubes and monitors.

Bill, was allowed to go into the room for 10 minutes alone. When he came out, he was in tears. "He asked me to please have Conway in a facility close to home so he could visit often," Carla said. Bill had thought that this was Conway's condition for the rest of his life. "I had to tell him we didn't know how Conway would be, but I assured him if it was the worst scenario, I would have him in the Louisville area." Bill sat down with Tony and Carla beside him as he cried "I never wanted him racing those damn cars anyway."

Conway, still in a coma found out about it for the first time when reading this book.

After I told Conway that Carla shared the story, a few weeks later he sent me an email with the following message.

Mark,

In my entire life I never saw my father get emotional about anything, ever. I never saw him shed a tear.

Conway gave me an example of his father's normally stoic exterior.

During the summer of 1964, the Wittens went on a road trip to visit family in another state. The family of five had to check into a motel once they arrived at their destination.

The hotel had a pool and the boys, ages 8 and 7 at the time, started begging Bill to take them swimming. Bill wasn't feeling well; he had just had a tooth pulled and was tired from the drive.

The boys continued to pester him until he agreed to take them swimming.

Once the three entered the pool area, Bill instructed the boys to stay on the shallow side of the pool. Just as he turned his back to sit down, the younger brother jumped into the deep portion of the pool and sank to the bottom. Bill jumped in, clothes and all, and retrieved the boy, who certainly would have drowned if not rescued. He then took both boys back to their room without a word.

"He didn't yell, he didn't cry, he didn't get mad, that's the way he was," said Conway.

So many flowers were sent to Conway during the first week, hospital management had to request only cards or letters be sent due to the lack of room. The flowers continued and were directed to other patients; staff members didn't have the heart to throw them away.

The hospital also fielded hundreds of telephone calls from many states and Canada. Carla was overwhelmed by the support and was very thankful; she needed it.

In the second week of his stay, doctors removed the endotracheal tube, (the artificial airway), to allow him to be ventilated and perform a tracheotomy. The endotracheal tube would damage the vocal cords if left in too long. Therefore, the tracheotomy was essential to breathe and promote healing and recovery if he could recover from the coma.

At the beginning of the third week, doctors started slowly bringing Conway out of the induced coma. They removed the tracheotomy tube but left the NG tube in place. When Conway reached a state of semi-consciousness, he started responding to voice commands and would squeeze Carla's hand when she spoke to him.

Doctors were able to run more tests at this point and found no permanent structural damage to Conway's skull. They met with Carla and told her she should make arrangements for a long-term care center; they didn't think Conway would improve beyond what they saw. Carla became angry and had several more discussions with the entire staff of doctors on Conway's case over the next couple of days. All but one told her his chances of improving were slim. She held on to that one doctor's optimism, which kept her going.

Throughout the waiting, Carla thought about the risks Conway took each time he got behind the wheel of a racecar. His parents had never approved of his racing; Conway was already racing when Carla met him and she knew how important it was to him. This was his fourth accident. What if he recovered and wanted to continue racing? How safe is the sport?

CHAPTER 8

SAFETY IN RACING

Conway's concern after the October 3, 1991 crash was safety. He mentioned to some of his closest friends that he needed more time to get used to the new car. It's relevant to give the reader, especially the reader not familiar with drag racing, a brief look at the history of safety in the sport.

The first commercial drag strip was formed in 1950 in Santa Ana, California, which also introduced the first official safety rules developed in part by Wally Parks, (for whom the famous Wally trophy is named) and the SCTA, the Southern California Timing Association. Those first mandated rules for vehicles and drivers were rudimentary and not very sophisticated; however, it was a starting point.

Drag racing became popular soon after World War II was over. Returning veterans were looking for excitement and making a car go faster than the factory intended had been around after the second car was built in the early 1900s. Illegal street racing was out of control by the late 1940s, and pioneers of the sport of organized drag racing began holding races on the dry lake beds located in southern California, in part to get the street racers off the street due to a severe increase in deaths among males in the 16 to 25 age bracket. Organizers wanted to prevent those fatalities.

Safety was a huge selling point for organized drag racing, and in 1951 Wally Parks formed the NHRA, the National Hot Rod Association. His goal was simple; to provide a safe place to race with safe drivers and race cars competing. Soon after, in 1956, the AHRA, American Hot Rod Association, was formed, and in 1970 the IHRA, International Hot Rod Association, was organized. Racing venues would become sanctioned by one of the three organizations if they could pass all the requirements of that organization, including the safety protocols. The association would grant a charter to track management after a representative physically inspected the site.

Although safety was the primary goal on the sanctioned tracks, it wasn't always the goal on non-sanctioned or "Outlaw Tracks" as they came to be known, especially in the sport's early days.

The Outlaw Tracks operated under their own protocol and didn't have to follow any organization's rules. Not all outlaw tracks ignored safety, but it was better organized on the larger sanctioned tracks.

According to the creators and editors of "Drag Racing Deaths," an internet-based page that lists the reported deaths of drag racers internationally since 1950, the following US numbers are listed. From 1950 to 2022, approximately 559 drag racers lost their lives due to accidents at the strip during competition or while testing. That number does not include international accidents or the deaths of fans, team and track workers, or the media caused by crashes, only the drivers.

This group uses multiple authentic sources from newspapers and other media to document their numbers; in addition, it isn't just the numbers; a story is written for each death explaining in as much detail as can be found what happened and why.

The first official drag racing death occurred on December 10, 1950, at the first commercial drag strip, at Santa Anna, California. The worst year was 1968, when 30 drivers died during the season. There were no deaths listed for drivers from 1951 through 1954, with the first double-digit number occurring in 1958. From 1955 to 2020, there was an average of 8 deaths per year while racing; in 2021, there were no deaths listed by drivers, in 2022, the most recent season as of this writing, eight drivers lost their lives while racing on drag strips.

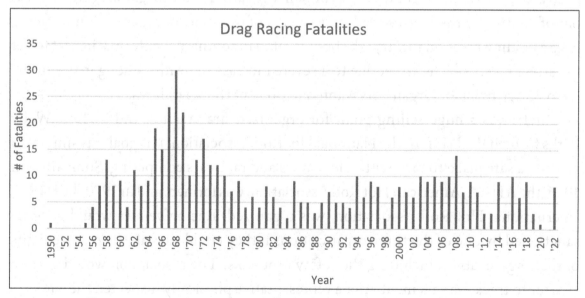

From 1950 to 2022, an estimated 559 drivers were killed in drag racing

During our research, we could not find any numbers listed for drivers injured while racing and survived. Using an industrial accident triangle, first developed by Herbert W. Heinrich in the 1930s, later updated by Frank Bird in the 1960s, and since edited by several researchers in the field of professional safety, shows us the relationship between one event causing a death, compared to events resulting in serious injury. According to the Frank Bird model, for every industrial death, there are ten severe injuries in the workplace. If we do the math and multiply 559 by 10, we get 5,590 severe injuries over 72 years. These numbers are just an estimate and only for drag racing drivers in the US.

As the facts show, in the first 18 years of commercial drag racing, the deaths increased nearly every year, as well as the mph of the vehicles. Even in the early years, speeds of 100 mph and above were typical. In 1964 Conrad "Connie" Kalitta became the first person to travel the quarter mile, 1.320 feet, at 200 miles an hour in a top fuel dragster. In 1994, some thirty years later, Kenny Bernstein set a new record of 300 mph in the quarter mile, and currently, as of this writing, the record stands at 338.94 mph set by Brittany Force on November 11, 2022. Top fuel dragsters are by far the fastest class, followed by Funny Cars and Pro Stockers.

Let's look at the facts again and understand that at 100 mph and faster, every safety precaution can be taxed when a driver loses control of the drag strip. At the incredible speeds the higher classes are going now; it's a coin toss as to the outcome of the driver's condition when there is an accident. Where does Conway's class compare in the top speed numbers? His car is capable of speeds over 180 mph in the quarter mile. Just picture this for a moment, 180 mpg in 7 seconds with an open cockpit, chrome molly frame, aluminum body, and an 800- horse fire breathing V8 sitting directly behind you just inches away.

In 1993 Conway's dragster had to meet the safety requirements in his class set by the NHRA. The following list identifies the majority of what was required in 1993 in order to race in Competition Eliminator:

➢ Driver- Must have a current and legal "competition" driver's license
➢ Driver restraint system- Three-inch- wide shoulder harnesses and lap belt. Two-inch- wide submarine belt and two-inch sternum belt. A device that releases the straps in one motion must be installed.
➢ The system must be replaced every two years.

➢ Racing helmet meeting the latest SFI rating (a certification that demonstrates that the manufacturer certifies the racing equipment has been laboratory tested to meet or exceed SFI safety specifications)
➢ Cushion in place behind the driver's head meeting NHRA standards.
➢ The driver must use an approved neck collar.
➢ Roll bar installed meeting specific NHRA standards and mandatory certification inspection every two years.
➢ Roll bars must be padded to meet specific NHRA standards.
➢ Fire-resistant body suit, face, and hand protection
➢ Braking parachute installed on all cars going 150 mph or faster from a recognized manufacturer.
➢ Rear wheel hydraulic disc brakes with iron or carbon fiber rotors.
➢ Rear engine dragsters:
➢ Deflector plate between cockpit and engine
➢ Approved transmission shield or blanket with flywheel shield of carbon fiber
➢ Wheelie bars meeting the required length for the class
➢ At each event, the racing vehicle is visually inspected by NHRA personnel before any testing, qualifying, or competitive racing to ensure that safety requirements are followed.

In the realm of safety, there are three stages of loss, pre-contact, contact, and post–contact. NHRA's post-contact controls include the work performed by the Safety Safari Team, first known as the Drag Safari in 1951. Just a small group of only four people then but as the sport grew, so did organize safety, and the Drag Safari became the Safety Safari.

In 1993 there were 18 national events (many more at the division and regional level) under the direction of the NHRA, which included scheduling, safety and technical issues, track preparation, and emergency response. As of this writing, the four-person team of the 1950s is now more than 100 full and part-time employees, not including contracted emergency service providers.

At each event, the NHRA has two fully equipped advanced life support ambulances on site, with a third ambulance minutes away on a call. A medical services center is located at the track with a doctor, nurse, and a team of paramedics. They also have a life-flight helicopter on standby if the need arises. The NHRA has two fully equipped trucks on site for firefighting and extrication purposes, with a team of trained firefighters and emergency response workers ready to respond immediately.

As technology improves, racing cars will go faster in all racing venues. The NHRA and other racing organizations such as NASCAR, responded to that concern; however, like most law or rule changes, it took an accident that resulted in death or severe injury to implement it.

After well- known driver Scott Kalitta died, ironically the son of Connie, in a Funny Car crash midseason 2008, NHRA management decided to shorten the competition distance for Top Fuel Dragsters and Funny Cars. Both classes use a use a nitro mixture for fuel, producing between 10 to 11 thousand horsepower at speeds over 300 mph in the 3 to the 4-second range. The track distance was shortened from 1,320 feet to 1,000, thus allowing an extra 320 feet for the cars to slow down. The average shutdown area for these cars is now approximately 1,700 feet.

In 1987 while racing on the superspeedway track of Talladega, Bobby Allison's car became air born at over 200 mph and crashed into the fencing between the spectators and the track. Although there were no fatalities, five spectators were injured, one seriously.

The following year, NASCAR, National Association for Stock Car Auto Racing, mandated that a restrictor plate, used to restrict airflow to the carburetor, be installed in order to slow the car s down on superspeedways.

In February of 2001, during the last lap of the Daytona 500, Dale Earnhardt crashed head-on into a wall killing him instantly due to a skull fracture.

By October, NASCAR mandated using the HANS device in each car. The HANS device prevents the head of the driver from snapping forward during a frontal impact.

Safety rule changes occur almost annually in most motorsports venues, and while all the changes aren't due to a tragic loss, the most significant rules changes are.

Carla's concerns about Conway continuing to race if he recovered were valid.

CHAPTER 9
SLOW RECOVERY, PERMANENT DISABILITIES

October 18, 1993

After 15 days in ICU, Conway was released from the Topeka hospital to a Louisville, Kentucky hospital. Carla contacted her insurance company about travel arrangements, and they refused to pay for a flight. The National Hot Rod Association arranged a flight for the couple to return home.

Conway was going back to Kentucky where he would be hospitalized for another ten days and then transferred to a rehab facility.

At the time, neither Conway nor Carla knew that a group of women in the Louisville area were including Conway in their prayers during bible study classes at the home of Terri Simmons. Six women met on Wednesday nights at various houses to study the bible and hold prayer sessions for people in need. "Once I saw the article in the paper about Conway, we prayed for him every week as a group. We were a group of prayer warriors," said Terri. "Prayer helps, studies show it, we prayed for Conway for months."

The most basic definition of prayer is "talking to God." Prayer is not meditation or passive reflection but a direct address to God. It is the communication of the human soul with the Lord who created the soul. Prayer is the primary way for believers to communicate their emotions, desires, and fellowship with Jesus and their God.

Author

In my early 40s, I became seriously ill with a rare blood illness and was transported by an ambulance from Elko, Nevada to the University of Utah Hospital in Salt Lake

City, Utah. During the following two weeks, I received transfusions of blood platelets in three hour procedures. After the tenth procedure they stopped for two days and rechecked my levels. My doctor informed me I was not responding, and he wanted to perform a surgical procedure that was very risky due to my condition.

I was frightened about the situation, and I turned to prayer to ease my mind. I refused the surgery, and the doctor had no choice but to continue the previous procedure.

After several more procedures my condition finally improved. My primary nurse came to my room on a Monday morning and, with a smile and a wink, told me I was being released after nearly a month in the hospital.

My doctor came in and was somber, explaining that he didn't know why the treatment had finally worked. He seemed somewhat perplexed with my case, but I wasted no time getting out of there and going home.

It took me another two weeks to gain my strength back and return to work, but during this period a good friend came by to see me. My friend looked at me and asked, "Do you have any idea how many people were praying for you?" He told me how many prayer chains, bible study classes, church groups, and individuals had been praying for my recovery; I was overcome with emotion and attended services at my church the following Sunday to give thanks. I learned the power of prayer through that ordeal. It is truly powerful medicine, so powerful!

Scientific research on praying goes back to the 1870s, and physician and researcher Larry Dossey, M. D., in his book "Prayer is Good Medicine," discusses how praying for oneself and others can scientifically heal illness and trauma. Most studies by other individuals and research groups come to the same conclusion; prayer works for whatever reason. Christians have known for a long time that prayer is essential in many ways, not just for the sick and injured but for anything they feel is important.

October 18 to November 2
Baptist East Hospital, Louisville, Kentucky

Conway was still in "guarded" condition with a trach and NG tube still in place, and he was receiving lung treatments to prevent pneumonia He was still lightly sedated as rest was a primary focus; He was unable to speak at the time and everyone thought it was due to all the procedures that had been done, the endless tubes up his nose and down his throat.

Also, Conway was still unable to walk and was having trouble swallowing. He would sometimes become restless, and try to move around.

Conway had always been a huge music fan; his record and CD collection were terrific, and he always played music in his vehicles while driving. One day Carla got an idea to bring in a portable music player, a "Boom Box" as they were called then. During Conway's uneasy and restless spells, she would play acoustic and other soft sounds like Neil Young's Harvest album for him, which almost always calmed him down. Carla had read how music helps recovering patients, and it worked on Conway.

Over the next three weeks, friends and family would shower the couple with support, including the members of DRAW, Drag Racing Association for Women, who offered to cook meals, do laundry, and even donate money. The benevolent fund that Bob Toy created was alive and well and through the help of hundreds of people, a benefit dance was held with all proceeds going to the Wittens as well as a benefit drag race held at Ohio Valley Raceway in Louisville, Kentucky.

Bob was also a great custodian of the fund. He sent Carla updates on all the money-raising transactions and a check for the proceeds.

Additional generous support was forthcoming. The owner of Farrell Trucking Company, where Conway worked, made a bold decision, as explained by the owner's son, Mike Farrell.

"Dad loved Conway, and due to his abilities on the job he decided to pay Conway the entire time he was off work." With Conway able to keep his job, he got to keep his insurance, too; without it, Carla and Conway would be in debt for the rest of their lives.

Traditionally, and primarily due to superstitions, most racers will not visit other racers hospitalized due to a racing accident. The same philosophy goes for a driver's death; most of his competitors will not attend funeral services. Conway had a few active drivers come to see him, but most sent cards and flowers, and some made phone calls. Mike Pustelny, friend, drag racer, and racing shop owner was one of the exceptions. He came to see Conway in Louisville shortly after he was admitted. Conway still had tubes running in and out of him and was semiconscious, unable to communicate.

Mike also brought along Dave, a drag racing friend from Canada. Dave took one look at Conway, turned around, walked out of the room, and refused to go back in.

In additional to friends and family wanting to see Conway, there were the curious and morbid that tried to get in to see him.

One day two male visitors came to the hospital asking to see Conway. The shift nurse had them wait at the desk while she returned to the room to talk to Carla. "There are two men here to see Conway. Would you like to talk to them?" Carla agreed and walked back to the desk with the nurse. She didn't recognize either man and when they introduced themselves, she didn't recognize their names. "I told both of them that I didn't know them and that they couldn't visit Conway."

With that said, both men started asking insensitive questions, like "We heard he only has half a head," said one man. The other man said, "He's just a vegetable now, right?" Carla became angry and demanded they both leave. "He will make a full recovery!" she yelled. Her last words to them as they walked away were, "AND DON'T COME BACK!"

There were rumors and stories about Conway's condition everywhere. One early bizarre rumor circulating was that Conway was wearing a "Prosthetics Face" due to damage caused by the accident. It certainly wasn't true but most felt that the Halloween season was affecting the rumors.

As his brain condition improved, his doctors reduced the number of meds he was receiving, and his comatose state slowly went away; soon, he would be released for concentrated rehabilitation.

October 31, 1993

Although he had been awake a few times over the past week, the following account of his first memories after the crash and what would be his first interaction with Carla is shared publicly for the first time. Conway still is unable to speak, so he writes in a notebook.

"The last thing I remember about Topeka was attending church services at the track on Sunday morning. I am in bed at Baptist East and the staff members are wearing costumes. I don't know where I'm at. I'm so woozy, the TV in my room is on, I think a talk show is airing, I dosed off again, and then suddenly there's a beautiful woman standing over me watching me sleep.

Conway: "Who are you?

Carla: "I'm Carla, your wife."

(Conway doesn't recognize her at first, and he's thinking, wow, she's pretty!)

Carla: "You wrecked the dragster in Topeka."

Conway: "How did I crash?"

Carla: "You barrel rolled it, you have a brain injury, and it will take time to heal."

Conway: "Who was I racing? Did I hit them?"

Carla: "Jeff Krug, you didn't hit him."

Carla: "I've been waiting for you to come out of the coma; I know you'll get better, but it will take time. I love you, Conway."

Conway heard her tell him that she loved him; her soothing voice, the look on her face, her touch was kind, and her devotion was apparent; he felt so blessed at the moment.

Bob Toy and his wife visited Conway just days before he was discharged from Louisville. After they left, Bob was somber and reflective. "It was apparent to me that Conway would never be able to race again, and I was sad that we would never know how far Conway could have gone with the new proposed partnership of Witten, Toy, and Holloway. It had a nice sound to it."

CHAPTER 10
FRAZIER REHABILITATION

November 1993 to December 1993

Frazier Rehab Institute was established as a physical rehabilitation institute in the early 1950's after Amelia Brown Frazier was injured in a car accident and had to travel out of state for services because none existed in Louisville at that time. The facility is classified as an "Acute Rehab" facility.

Acute rehab is intense rehab for patients who have experienced a major medical trauma and will not be able to fully recover without the aid of intense therapy and medical assistance or would or be able to recover in a reasonable amount of time. Some patients may have had a stroke, just come out of major surgery, had head trauma, had an amputation, or may still be dealing with a serious illness. Most of these patients will not be able to fully recover without the aid of intense therapy and medical assistance or would not be able to recover in a reasonable amount of time. Acute care patients usually come straight from the hospital, opening up hospital beds for patients who need medical help, an acute stay is usually not long, since the "acute" portion of the rehab moves to a lower stage of rehab when the patient is progressing. The acute care patient has 3-5 hours of therapy every day, with a mix of speech, physical, occupational, respiratory or electromagnetic therapies. They are seen by a physician, or a team of physicians, every day to mark progress and make recommendations for continuation of rehabilitation. Acute patients are expected to make fast progress and move up a level out of acute rehab.

Conway would spend the next six weeks at this facility and was able to go home most weekends with Carla after he learned to walk again. At first, he was confined to a wheelchair at all times unless there was a care provider with him to help.

His physical therapist was Lynn Person, whose father was the athletic director at the University of Louisville.

"She was a very patient and caring therapist," said Conway. "She would do simple things for me that I'm sure were monotonous to her but helped me tremendously."

His occupational therapist was Kim Hicks helped him brush his teeth, get dressed and so on. "I was somewhat embarrassed getting dressed and undressed in the audience of a young woman, but I had no control over it" mentioned Conway. "That place would take all your pride and throw it out the door."

A perfect example of this was when he was having trouble with constipation during his first few days at the facility. One night a rather large female nurse and Carla came to his room and announced that that he was going to get an enema. "I was mortified," said Conway. "I was sitting on the portable toilet when the nurse got on her knees and stuck this tube up my butt." I felt violated and I could see Carla snickering in the background, I felt that they were getting some type of revenge."

By now another nurse had entered the picture and the three of them told Conway to just be patient while the liquid was pumped into his colon. It didn't take long and Conway, embarrassed to the point of trauma, looked at the three women and said "Now?" The Nurses nodded yes and he let the backed up load flow while they watched. "If that doesn't make you lose all your inhibitions, nothing will" laughed Conway.

His bed at Frazier rehab was equipped with a sensor that detected any moisture. If he had an "accident," the sensor would go into alarm, and a nurse or aid would immediately be notified. Conway wasn't having any of these issues, but the sensor was still occasionally going off, apparently malfunctioning.

One night the sensor alarm went off, and a male nurse came to his room to check on the situation. After feeling for wetness and finding none, the nurse angrily said, "I'll fix this damn thing!" Grabbing the sensor connection in his hand, the male nurse violently ripped the wires out of it, thus permanently disabling the alarm.

"Now you just get some rest, Conway," he said.

One routine that Conway did fear was a nightly injection of the drug Heparin. Heparin is an anticoagulant and is used to prevent harmful clots from forming in blood vessels. In Conway's case it would aid in the reduction of inflammation in his brain and was injected in his stomach, which was very painful.

Conway's first trip home after the accident was memorable. "Carla brought me into the house and I was still having memory issues. As I looked around I was thinking, "Wow, this is a really nice place, I wonder who owns it!"

For weeks Conway was 'foggy,' an odd feeling he had while he was still regaining his memory. There were funny episodes and many sad ones. There were visits from friends when he didn't recognize them, other times he would. It was a frustrating time.

Every morning at Frazier was the same routine for Conway, breakfast in a common room with other head injury patients where they would talk about the day, the weather, the time, events of the season, their families; topics like this helped their thinking process.

After breakfast, therapy would begin; occupational, physical and speech therapy. All the therapy sessions were held in a huge basement floor facility and the patients would be transported there in their wheel chairs using an elevator.

An example of physical therapy for Conway consisted of wading into a swimming pool with a moveable floor, an exercise to help him regain his ability to walk.

The sessions went on all morning with a lunch break and then all afternoon right up to the evening meal.

Gale Powley was once again living and working in the area and offered to help Carla with transporting Conway to and from doctor visits and home, leaving Carla free to work her at her job. Gale had a loose schedule and was happy to help in any way. This turned out to be extremely helpful to the family.

"One day Conway had a visitor; it was businessman Jesse Ballew. Conway knew Jesse from the days when he owned Ohio Valley Raceway as well as when he was a customer at the racing engine shop and friend to Mike Keown. "Jesse is a deeply religious man and when he found out I had been hurt he came to pray for me." Jesse stood by Conway's bed and prayed with him for several minutes. "I will always be grateful to him for thinking of me."

The average time spent in a facility like this is two weeks, after four weeks Conway was walking again on his own, but he needed advanced speech therapy and other services. His next step was subacute rehab.

Conway was released from Frazier Rehab in the on December 20th and would move on to his next challenge.

Lakeshore Rehabilitation Center, Birmingham, Alabama, December 1993 to April 1994

Subacute rehab is a level lower than acute rehab in terms of intensity. If progress continues steadily in subacute rehab, the stay is usually more extended than in acute rehab.

Carla researched several subacute facilities as close to Louisville as possible. She narrowed her choices to two facilities, Duke University Rehabilitation Institute in Durham, North Carolina, and Lakeshore Rehabilitation Center in Birmingham, Alabama. Conway's part-time crew member and family friend Gordon Holloway knew Bobby Allison, the famous NASCAR driver who was involved in a career-ending crash in 1988. Carla contacted Judy Allison, Bobby's wife, and Judy gave Carla a detailed account of how great the care was at Lakeshore. Carla decided on Lakeshore, and they agreed to fly her round trip from Louisville to Birmingham every weekend to see Conway.

Lakeshore Rehabilitation Center in December of 1993 was a private rehab facility and the leading provider of inpatient rehabilitation for stroke, brain injury, and other complex neurological and orthopedic conditions. They provided a personalized care plan using clinical collaboration and advanced technologies to meet Conway's unique needs and help him achieve his goals.

Their inpatient rehabilitation hospital used an interdisciplinary team approach that included physical, speech, and occupational therapists, rehabilitation physicians, on nurses, case managers, dietitians, and more, combined with their advanced technology and expertise.

On December 15, 1993, Conway checked in to Lakeshore, where he would remain for four months. He received six hours of therapy five days per week under the constant care of registered nurses. The two main areas of concentration for Conway were walking and speech.

One of the physical therapists working with Conway would become very special to both him and Carla. Her name was Denette and she was amazing.

"She could motivate Conway into doing painful exercises that eventually helped him to walk again." Denette would work with Conway in the swimming pool at the center, encouraging him to step it up and do more. She was an exceptional person.

The following week Carla took Conway back to Louisville for Christmas. They flew in on the evening of December 23. He was still using a wheelchair but making progress.

As they drove, he noticed the bridges and the buildings in the Louisville area were decorated with Christmas lights. This stirred his feelings, and he started talking, trying to describe something to Carla. His speech was still seriously affected very similar to a stroke victim. Carla could pick up a word or two but she couldn't understand what Conway was saying. He would mumble something or other and then point to the sky. Finally, after several attempts, Carla understood what he was saying: "How did they get me down?"

Carla was confused and didn't understand, and Conway was frustrated because he couldn't speak clearly. Again, he asked, "How did they get me down? There were bright lights."

Carla figured Conway was still a little woozy from all the treatment and all the excitement. She later forgot about it, but Conway didn't. He had much more to say; he just couldn't organize the thoughts in his mind yet.

January 16, 1994

The holidays were over and Carla was settling into a routine, every weekend she would fly to Birmingham to see Conway. On one Saturday morning, when she got to the center, Conway was excited to tell her something, Gordon Holloway was visiting, too, and both were in the room.

For the first time, Conway had prepared a written description of his experience and handed it to Carla. As she read it, she said Conway was pointing to the sky.

"I found myself in a place where you talk without a mouth, hear without ears, and see without eyes. It was a totally spiritual place; it was so calming. I felt like it was the most comforting place I had ever been. Time doesn't exist. A voice was there. I started to ask the voice questions in my typical cynical way.

"Where am I?"

The voice said, "You are with the Father." The language wasn't English, but I understood every word.

I then asked the voice, "Where am I going?"

The voice said, "To Heaven."

I said, "I've been so bad in this life."

The voice said, "I came to earth as Jesus Christ; anyone that believes in me will go to Heaven and be with me."

I felt the voice knew that I believed in Jesus Christ, and I said, "All right." I then asked the voice, "Which religion is the right religion?"

The voice said, "There is no right or wrong religion as long as it teaches about Jesus Christ."

I got the impression that the voice liked arguing about religion.

The voice said, "How can anyone say that a person like Billy Graham or Mother Theresa is bad?"

"In the car back in December, I didn't know what he was saying; after reading what he had written down, I understood it," said Carla. "I was shaken at first; it made the risk of him almost losing his life even more real. I couldn't help but recall the days he was in ICU, and we didn't know what would happen. I was raised a Baptist, and I am a believer, so I believed what he had written down was true and that he had experienced it. I told him he had a reason to be alive and that there was something for him to fulfill in his life. I wanted him to believe that."

There was so much going on in both Conway's and Carla's life at that time neither had the time to follow up on what it all meant. Did Conway have a near-death experience? That topic would be secondary in their lives for the next several years. There was so much to overcome, and neither knew what was next.

Conway grew more vigorous and fitter as the months passed, but it was hard to understand when he spoke. He was working hard in speech therapy but with little progress.

"I flew in one weekend, and it was close to Valentine's Day," Carla commented. "I walked into Conway's room, and there was a huge balloon bouquet with a card attached; my name was on the card." Somehow Conway had convinced one of his therapists to purchase the gift because Conway wasn't allowed off the property due to his condition at the time. Conway paid the therapist back, and Carla was thrilled with the present. "It was a great surprise and so sweet of him to do!" said Carla.

The following April, doctors at Lakeshore were ready to release Conway. First, paperwork was completed for CJ Farrell, Conway's employer, regarding his job responsibilities versus his current disabilities. The therapists needed to know what would be expected when he returned to work, and the trucking company also needed to know what to expect. Next, the couple had an exit interview with doctors and staff.

Conway was officially diagnosed with "Developmental Dysarthria," a motor speech disorder caused by a traumatic brain injury. He had overcome the swallowing disorder and had learned to walk again, although he had a slight limp and his range of walking motion was affected. His overall health was good, but he would need time to get back in shape concerning daily tasks and might experience fatigue. The doctors warned him that another blow to the head might be fatal, and racing was out of the question.

He would continue speech therapy in Louisville at Frasier, but doctors were apprehensive about him regaining his speech completely, but Conway wasn't.

During his stay at Lakeshore, he met the one and only Bobby Allison, the NASCAR driver from the famous Allison family. Bobby had been through the program a few years earlier due to his own career-ending crash. During the 1988 Miller High Life 500, Allison crashed head-on into a barrier and then was t-boned on the driver's side of the car. It took 30 minutes for Bobby to be extracted from the wreck, and then he was rushed to the ER. When he arrived, doctors declared him dead but moments later realized he was still breathing. He was rushed into surgery, where a decompressive craniectomy procedure was performed. After surviving that, he spent the next six weeks in intensive care, and did his subacute rehab at Lakeshore spending several months there. Bobby attended a function at Lakeshore while Conway was there, and they were introduced to each other. Bobby told him it had taken him two years to learn to speak again, encouraging Conway to continue with therapy.

Another part of the exit interview was the lengthy material on depression and suicide, and according to the data presented to them, the risks of depression in people with a TBI increased significantly, but it was the suicide information that was alarming. The risk of suicide thoughts increased with TBI persons, and the suicide rate was double compared to people without TBI. Conway and Carla read and discussed all the information, not knowing that each issue would affect them in the months and years ahead.

They also received counseling about marital issues due to TBI. "They bombarded us with this information; it was almost like we didn't stand a chance of making it because of my injury," mentioned Conway.

The last issues that were discussed were potential personality changes that TBI people experience. On average they exhibit extended periods of frustration and anger easier, both traits are completely out their control due to the injury, and it takes time for them to adjust and correct the behavior.

Conway went home to Louisville in April of 1994 to start his life with the two handicaps he would deal with for the rest of his life; his speech impediment, and walking. Although the walking issue slowed him down, the speech issue would prove to be his biggest challenge.

The Witten's insurance plan had covered 99 percent of the estimated two million dollar medical costs incurred due to the accident, and thanks to the trucking company continuing to pay his salary along with all the donations and Carla's salary, the Wittens were financially stable.

Conway did chores around the house to get his body back in shape. He mowed the lawn, and did other odd jobs around the house. He also retested and got his driver's license renewed, which gave him a little more freedom. He was ready to go back to work.

CHAPTER 11
THE DARK DAYS

April 1994 to March 1999

In late April of 1994, Conway returned to work part-time on the day shift at the trucking company. He was used to managing the company on a shift by himself, but now, due to his speech issues, he was sharing responsibilities with another person.

"At first, I was just getting back into the swing of things, trying to manage my part of the responsibilities," said Conway. He would come home frustrated at times because the communication issue was challenging. "He couldn't talk on the phone, and most of the time, he had to write out a command or an answer on a yellow pad he carried with him," mentioned Carla.

May 1994, NHRA Points Race, Indianapolis, Indiana

For the first time in seven months, Conway was at the races but this time only as a spectator. As he walked the pits saying hello to many of his former competitors, the announcer at the track, Leo Taugher, gave Conway a warm welcome over the PA system. A photographer for the weekly newspaper, NHRA National Dragster, took Conway's picture, and it appeared on the cover the following week.

Conway had mixed emotions about being at the track. In one way, he wanted everyone to know he was recovering, and in other ways, the competitor in him was yearning to get behind the wheel of a fast race car and make a run.

As 1994 continued, Conway kept working but his mental challenges and communication difficulties proved to be very frustration. This led him to become argumentative, which led to some confrontations. In addition he wasn't getting along with the co-supervisor.

89

January 1995

One day in mid January, Conway pulled into his driveway and opened the garage door. Carla's car was already there, which was atypical; she usually worked late. He thought she must be sick, or something had happened. Carla met him at the door.

"What's wrong?" Conway asked.

"Mr. Farrell called," she said. "I'm sorry to have to tell you this, but they're letting you go."

The news hit him like a shotgun blast, he became upset and very emotional. He had already lost so much: his race car, the ability to speak, nearly losing his life, and now his job? He had worked for this company for over ten years and had been promoted several times. He had an excellent work record.

Hadn't they paid his salary while he was in the hospital and during rehabilitation? You just don't do that for everyone, only the ones that contribute. To top it off, the Farrell's were not just his employer. They not only worked together, but raced, celebrated milestones together, they were like family. To Conway, this news was confusing as well as devastating.

"They called me to spare a scene at work. It would have been a bad experience to have him getting upset at work in front of everyone and then driving home," said Carla.

Conway didn't see it like that; he was devastated over losing his job. He was also beyond angry, and felt it was the single worst event in his life, outside the accident. Although he told no one, for years it gnawed at him daily; the rage was sometimes overwhelming.

Although never diagnosed, he had symptoms of post-traumatic stress disorder, which is very common with TBI. He became easily aggravated, had little patience, and held it all inside because of an admitted macho pride. He never sought help from family members or professional services to overcome these issues because the TBI also affects a sufferer's judgment. Adding to his stress was yet another letdown; this one was just as bad and sent him into a more profound depression.

"Many people asked me why I didn't return to building engines and head cylinder work. I tried. I returned to Mike Keown's shop, and he put me to work. I wasn't there long, though; I think someone was uncomfortable with my handicap, and Mike finally let me go soon after I started claiming there wasn't enough work," said Conway.

Conway was slowly withdrawing from everything in his life. He needed a break.

April to October 1995

The break he was looking for came in the form of a community re-entry program held at a Frazier Rehab satellite facility. For six months, Conway participated in activities that would help him find a new career.

A day in the life for Conway during this period consisted of speech therapy, computer training, and other classes. When not in recovery, Conway did the grocery shopping, housework, and yard work; he even prepared meals. "I was a regular house husband for a while, and I didn't mind it," mentioned Conway. "It helped my demeanor but only temporarily."

In October, he enrolled at Ivy Tech in Sellersburg, Indiana. He would be learning Cad /Cam, a course that introduces the student to the foundational knowledge of computer-aided design, manufacture, and the practical use of CNC machines. A direction that he thought was interesting.

Conway was celebrating his 40th birthday, but he had nothing to cheer about if the truth were known. He hid many hurtful issues, and getting up in the morning was a chore.

Some people have poker faces; they can fool you just with their actions and demeanor; Conway was the ultimate pro at this.

He was embarrassed at his failures, hurt by the circumstances, allowing his pride to dictate and override his common sense. When asked why he didn't reach out for help, he can only shake his head and say, "I was lost and didn't know what to do." His father had just been diagnosed with cancer to add to his stress.

December 1995

Although Conway was in school, these were dark days for the Wittens. He was frustrated with his life, angry about the situation, and falling into a depressed state. So was Carla.

By December, he was on the brink of disaster, and all the signs were there.

"I just couldn't handle the disappointment in my life. I knew I had changed and I couldn't get my old life back," said Conway. One week before Christmas, Conway was crossing the Sherman Minton Bridge into Indiana. "The snow was piled up on the sides of the bridge and I kept thinking about driving into the side and through the bridge. Three times I steered towards the side, and then I caught myself steering back." Finally, once across the bridge he pulled off the main road, stopped, and broke down crying, not knowing what would happen next.

Conway never shared his suicidal thoughts with Carla. He didn't want her to worry; she had gone through enough. Conway also put his near-death experience on the back burner. "I had to finish school, I needed to work, and there was a lot of pressure on me," he said.

Carla had done her homework and got Conway's rehab and schooling paid for through a Vocational Rehab grant, a huge blessing since Conway was out of work. For the next two and a half years, Conway attended school, both day and some night classes, and remained a house husband while Carla worked full time at the bank. "I took some tough classes after I got core subjects out of the way. Some of the math was so difficult that the instructor would allow us to take tests home to complete them," said Conway.

Spring 1998

Conway graduated in the spring of 1998 with an associate degree in Mechanical AutoCAD Drafting without missing a single day of classes. "The school didn't offer a bachelor's degree, and I needed to go work," said Conway. It didn't take long; he had a job in less than a week.

Conway started as a temp editing Auto Cad drawings for a local company. One month later, he landed a full-time position with a cable TV company drafting maps; the only downfall was the 5 pm to 2 am hours.

Conway would go home, sleep until 10 am, then get up, and head to a body shop his friend owned to work on a Corvette he was restoring. He got a good deal on the 'Vette and performed most of the restoration, languidly performing himself. It kept him occupied and helped with his depression.

He remained on this schedule for the next several months. Carla's work hours were 9 am to 5 pm, but she always worked late and usually was home by six or 6:30. The couple wouldn't see each other during the week at all, and on weekends their situation could have been more comfortable. "I knew we were growing apart; we hardly spoke to each other," said Conway.

March 17, 1999

Conway woke up around ten and found Carla home. He approached her as she sat on the couch. "Why are you home?" Carla told him she was leaving. "I love you but I'm not in love with you, Conway. I'll be in touch." With that, Carla walked out.

Carla drove to Mike Keown's shop and told him what was happening. "He's going to need his friends now more than ever."

"You always wished there was something you could have done differently. We always seemed to be reaching for something more and were both motivated. He was reaching for top honors in racing, to be a champion and nationally recognized. I was trying to get an education and then a good job."

Carla confessed that the marriage was in trouble before the accident. She was lonely and somewhat frustrated; over the years, seeing each other only on the run had taken its toll. Both of them worked multiple jobs, school day and night, traveling every weekend during the racing season. Even when she went with him, most of the time they were not together because the crew and Conway were focused on racing. "This wasn't a hobby, it was his life. I didn't fit in at the track," said Carla. "I'm not blaming anyone because this was just how it was. It took a toll on me, although I tried hard to adjust."

After the accident, there was no one braver or stronger than Carla. She made sure Conway was taken care of; she kept a close eye on the people that were providing care, getting in their faces when she knew they had made mistakes. She handled the insurance; applied for grants and any other monetary help she could find to help them financially. Carla was determined to get Conway the best therapy and rehab she could find. She flew to several cities and spent hours on the phone researching the best care. She flew to Alabama practically every weekend while Conway was there for rehab, and in the meantime, she was not only holding down a job but excelling at it, receiving numerous promotions, up to a manager-level position. Carla was a rock, but it significantly affected her physically, mentally, and emotionally. The dynamics of her marriage to Conway had changed.

"By the time Conway was out of school and working again, I felt more like an advocate than a wife. I was having trouble concentrating at work, I wasn't sleeping, something had to give," said Carla.

Carla was seeing a counselor in both private and group sessions. "I felt guilty about attending the sessions because they were expensive, but I was struggling, and it helped me," she commented. "I want to be clear that neither the counselor nor anyone in the group was trying to convince me to leave Conway; I made that decision alone. You can't talk to friends and family about some things, and I didn't want them jaded, and I also felt uncomfortable talking about it with them."

Carla was nearing 40, she wasn't happy, but she didn't blame Conway. For her the marriage was over. She went to her sister's, exhausted, confused, and depressed. Her sister called their brother, now a Pastor, and he came over to talk.

Conway had known the marriage was in trouble for a long time. "I was expecting it to happen, I was so down and depressed, and I just couldn't communicate," said Conway. He did his best to keep his composure, although it had been a very trying and confusing six years since the accident. Conway shares his thoughts about the marriage ending.

"I realize now that I was selfish at times, self-driven; I made other mistakes too. As wrong as it was, that was my demeanor at the time. I was contemplating suicide because I had lost so much and was feeling sorry for myself.

Carla went above and beyond for me while I was recovering; she was strong and caring. No, I don't blame Carla now, I wish things would have been different, but it took a long time for me to forgive, and I have; I hope Carla has forgiven me."

Carla moved in with a lady friend during the separation, and Conway remained in the house. By summer, the house was sold, the divorce was final in August and both had moved on. Carla continued counseling for two more years after the divorce.

On October 30, Conway's father passed away after a four-year illness, the last six months in a nursing home; he was 77. Carla attended the services, and she commented on her relationship with Bill. "I was close to Bill; he had a great sense of humor and always made me laugh."

Conway moved into an apartment in the Ferncreek area of Louisville and went to day shift hours on his job. He could get through the day alright, but during the night, consistently alone for the first time in eighteen years; his state of mind began to deteriorate. There had been so many changes in his life in the last six years he couldn't comprehend it all.

One night, alone with his thoughts, it all hit him like a delayed reaction. He broke down, unable to control his emotions. He had never experienced a point so low in his life; he felt helpless, alone, scared, and without hope. Once again, he contemplated suicide.

"That was without a doubt the worst night of my life," Conway remembers. Now, when he hears the Aaron Lewis song "I lost it all," it reminds him of that night, and he can't help it, he always sheds a tear.

"I lost it all; I tried to make it through my pain
I lost it all, and it'll never be the same
And right now the only thing that's left, is sadness and the sham
I lost it all, and it'll never be the same
I lost it all."

CHAPTER 12
THE SEARCH FOR A NEW BEGINNING

During that night, so dark and filled with loss, Conway calmed himself down, took inventory of the situation, and decided, "I need God back in my life!" At his lowest and most vulnerable point, he began to pray.

People will say that seeking or renewing religious faith when you are vulnerable is a sign of weakness, maybe even selfishness. Everyone's situation is different in their acceptance or even denial of religion. But Conway believes his vulnerability at that moment was his willingness to present himself without self-protection authentically.

Conway wanted the world to know about his near death experience and all the facts that led up it. He just didn't know how to do it. He was still confused.

Conway's spiritual walk thus far needed to be more consistent. He was undoubtedly a believer in God and believed that Christ was the savior. He had struggled not in his belief but in practice. As a young man, he attended a Baptist Church occasionally, mostly with friends.

After his marriage to Carla, they would attend Christmas and Easter services together annually, but no more than that. Then in 1987, he began to participate in nondenominational services at the drag strip on Sunday mornings when he was racing.

Conway's paternal Grandfather was a devout Methodist, and this had left an impression on him. Later in 1987, he decided to attend a Methodist Church during a Sunday service and enjoyed the environment.

He had felt the need to pursue his faith, but convinced himself he didn't have the time while working an average of 15 hours daily at jobs, working on his race car in between, and grabbing sleep when he could. During the racing season, nearly every weekend was spent at the drag strip, and in the off season, he picked up extra shifts at the race shop or worked on his car.

The only day he had off was Sunday when he wasn't racing. Sunday was a "sleep-in day." We can't forget Carla was also working three jobs at times, going to school at all hours in between; Sunday was a day to rest, literally.

Conway had tried to make sense of the experience he had explained to Carla in the car one night and then to Carla and Gordon together in his room at the rehab center in Alabama.

Conway had always felt that he was meant to share his near death experience and all the facts that led up to it. He just didn't know how to do t.

In his first attempt to speak with clergy about his near-death experience, Conway approached a Methodist Minister around 1997.

During this meeting, the Minister read the narrative that Conway had written down. He asked if he had ever been baptized.

"No, I haven't," said Conway.

Within a week, Conway was baptized, and his NDE was shared with all the Church members. He started attending this Church every Sunday, alone.

Fern Creek Methodist Church, summer of 2000

Due to his move across the bridge, his next Church was in the Fern Creek area of Louisville, the Fern Creek Methodist Church.

After Conway shared his near-death experience and racing career with church members that summer, a few approached him with an idea. "Why don't you write a book about it, Conway?" More than one person mentioned it, and Conway told them he would consider it. That evening Conway sat in silence thinking about the possibility of a book. Maybe that was it? A book has the potential to reach the world. "My goal was to let as many people know about the facts of my NDE as possible." Conway went to his computer and started writing.

Conway continued working for the cable TV company and was still restoring the Corvette at a slow but steady pace and slowly things began to improve,

Conway met and started a new relationship with a woman that lived in the same complex he did. Her name was Susan Anderson, a widow about Conway's age, and worked as a CPA. She was also a Catholic. Although Conway and Susan had different religious faiths, it didn't interfere with their relationship. Susan found Conway intelligent, attractive, and very mechanically handy, and she didn't seem to mind his speech and walking handicaps. Conway found Susan beautiful, funny, and engaging.

After dating for a year he fell in love with Susan, and she was in love with him. They exchanged vows and soon moved to a new home.

Conway had shared his near-death experience with Susan and the idea of a book before they were married. Susan didn't respond; it seemed she initially had no interest in it. This puzzled Conway, but he didn't push the subject.

Conway changed jobs several times over the next few years, finally returning to the engine machining business. He once again lost sight of the near-death experience and book and was somewhat reluctant to follow up due to Susan's indifference. He would try to write on occasion and became flustered; he just didn't know how to put it all down on paper.

In 2012 Conway went to work at Atlas Machining, a company that did engine machining work on a national level. Conway joined the company in the cylinder head department, and within two years, he was nearly running that part of the business. Management at the company loved him, incorporated his knowledge and skills, and grew because of him.

One day while at her mother's home, Susan brought up Conway's near-death experience. Upon hearing the story for the first time, Susan's mother, a devout Roman Catholic, quickly rejected the story as a vivid dream, possibly even drug-induced due to Conway's injury. She was adamant about her feelings, and Susan admitted that she felt the same way but didn't want to hurt Conway's feelings.

Her mother suggested that no matter the outcome, Susan should be honest with Conway and let him know her real feelings about it.

Soon after, Susan approached Conway and shared her conversation with her mother, and that she shared her mother's belief that the experience was a dream. Conway, defensive and with conviction, told her it was certainly not a dream and to drop the subject. He was angry but didn't want the issue to cause trouble in their marriage because several other things had been building up between them lately. Conway decided not to share some of the memoirs he had been occasionally working on. For now, it would remain his secret.

Later in the year, Rich Gimmel, the owner of Atlas, who had gotten to know Conway personally, thought his story would make an excellent article, so he contacted a friend that was a reporter for the local paper. "Look, I have a handicapped fellow working here, the experience and knowledge he brought to our shop has changed how we do business, this guy is just awesome, and he has an interesting story behind the handicaps." After he finished explaining, the reporter thought so too.

A few weeks later, an excellent story about Conway appeared in the Louisville paper entitled, "A passion for engines led this employee to Atlas." The article was well written and started with Atlas management praising Conway's work, attitude, and personality; he had changed their process in the cylinder head shop.

Atlas's Shop supervisor, Leonard Nett, discussed Conway's skills and work ethic. The reporter listed his drag racing accomplishments at the national level and his collection of Wallys and national records. The story continues with his accident, near-death experience, faith, and beliefs. The following is the last paragraph in the article.

"Today, Conway reflects a positive outlook about life at work and when he is home with his wife, Susan. And above all else, Conway is filled with gratitude. He is thankful "not to worry about what will happen after death." He also wants others to know "there is a place already paid for, and God welcomes us with open arms."

The night the article ran was a miserable evening in the Witten home. Susan read it and came unglued. "What in the world were you thinking, Conway?" she said.

"My name is in that article; my friends, my mother, everyone will see it." She was upset to the extreme, but Conway was unrepentant. "It's the truth, Susan, the truth! It happened, and I'm not going to hide it."

The couple went to bed that night, bewildered and angry at each other.

August 19, 2015

Malcolm "Mike" Keown, 70, passed away on August 19, 2015. A portion of his obituary is as follows:

> Mike was a Super Stock Drag Racing World Champion and the owner of Mike Keown Racing, which specialized in Super Stock Racing Engines. In times of relaxation, he loved fishing, boating, and being outdoors. Mike was also a member of West Maple Street Baptist Church.

On Saturday, August 22, Conway's long time friend, employer, and racing partner was laid to rest in Jeffersonville, Indiana. Conway attended the services, saw some old friends, and went home to reminisce about all the times he had spent with Mike over the years. It was a sad day.

The Corvette Conway had been restoring for several years was now ready. Conway drove it a little, took it down the local drag strip to see what it would do, and then put it up for auction. The car sold for a good price and Conway put the money down on a Shelby Daytona kit car. He planned to build the car himself to drive and show. He knew the history of the original cars and loved the body style.

The Shelby Daytona Cobra Coupe was engineered and purpose-built for racing competition in GT Division Three venues, including 12-hour and 24-hour races on the International Championship for GT Manufacturers. There were only six cars built between 1964 and 1965.

Carroll Shelby asked employee Pete Brock to design Daytona's aerodynamic bodywork and Bob Negstad to create the car's suspension. Driver Ken Miles helped road test the first car built at the Shelby American race shop in Venice, California. The remaining five were built at Carrozzeria Gran Sport in Modena, Italy.

All six cars survived their racing history and are held in private collections. The price paid recently for car number 4 was 7.5 million dollars.

A huge argument ensued over Conway's kit car purchase and over the next few months Conway and Susan's marriage continued to deteriorate to the point of no return.

Conway left late in the summer and moved in with his mother. The divorce was final before the end of the year.

CHAPTER 13
HALL OF FAME

In 2016 Conway was notified by representatives of the Kentucky Motorsports Hall of Fame that he had been selected for induction. He was invited to the ceremony and asked to give a speech.

Founded in 2008 by Bobby Davis and P.O. Brown, the Kentucky Motorsports Hall of Fame and Museum is located in Central City, Kentucky. The group displays the following "Mission Statement" on their web site;

"Our mission is to honor an individual, family, or team who has merited recognition and distinction by public accomplishments and contributions regarding Kentucky motorsports history and will serve as an inspiration and example of the highest traditions and reputation that will withstand the test of time."

Each year the selection committee chooses eight individuals through a review and balloting process. The committee, made up of former racers, racing team members, and historians, handles the selection process after reviewing hundreds of applications annually. The purposes of the nominations are as follows:

To preserve the racing history of Kentucky and the region and honor those, living or dead, who by achievement have produced a lasting contribution to Kentucky motorsports heritage.

Some of the more nationally known inductees in the hall include Dale Funk, Army Armstrong, Darrell Alderman, Butch Krieger, Jack Roush, Michael Waltrip, Mark, Jeff, and David Green.

When Conway received his notice, he was thrilled. He had no knowledge that he had been nominated, let alone voted on and approved. Members of the selection committee informed Conway that they wanted to meet with him before the formal presentation so he could share the details of his career-ending accident and his near-death experience with them personally. He wrote it out and gave it to Bob Toy, his long-time friend, who also had the honor of reading his acceptance speech due to Conway's speech impairment.

After the accident details were read, Bob shared the following, once again written by Conway, with the committee.

"Over the past twenty-three years, it's been my quest to share my near-death experience with as many people willing to listen, including the press, my church, family and friends, and now you, members of the Kentucky Motorsports Hall of Fame selection committee. Not everyone believes me when I give them the details. I've been teased about it while some people tell me I was dreaming, others have even been angry with me, but as God is my witness, the experience was real."

After Bob read the NDE details, Conway included the following.

"I want you to think back on your life. Think of the best moment or moments you have ever experienced. For me, the near-death experience was four times greater than anything I had ever experienced, it was a utopia, and it was completely, without question, a peacefulness you have never experienced. There was no sense of time, no worry, a feeling of love. I didn't want to leave it, and now I do not fear death."

The selection committee members were initially silent as if taking it all in and picturing it in their minds. They thanked both Bob and Conway and left the room, many with a sense of fulfillment.

Later that same day Bob Toy read Conway's prepared speech at the formal presentation to the committee members, other inductees, and the public in attendance. Here's a portion of that speech:

"Where do I start? I owe so much to many people; I earned this as a team effort and accepted it as a team award."

Conway told the group about meeting Tony Clark and his first time at a drag strip, his early days drag racing the Mustangs, moving on to the Corvette, the Olds, the Camaro, and the dragsters. He told several humorous stories that happened during his twenty years racing, and the list of people he thanked is included below:

Chuck Belanger, Carla, Mike Keown, Gordon Holloway, Russ, Jack, Craig, and Helen Krammer, Kevin and Dale Gentry, Jim Powers, Kenny Morris, Rick Fuller, Donnie Daniels, CJ and Mike Farrell, Joe Williamson, Bill, Wanda, Paul Decker, Jim, and Jimmy DeFrank, and Mike Pustelny.

He will be forever remembered as a significant contributor to drag racing in Kentucky, and fittingly, his mother was in attendance holding a tissue to her face.

Two years later Wanda Witten passed away suddenly of a heart ailment; she was 86. Most people knew of her artistic side; she painted ceramics and wooden crafts, she was one of the best cooks around, and she was a hard worker at home and on the job. Carla reminisced about Wanda and shared her thoughts.

"I went to visit her shortly after Bill passed away. We went on a long walk, and I told her about what happened in my marriage with Conway. It was a pleasant visit and we laughed about some of the funnier moments we had shared. I hugged her goodbye when I left. I loved both of Conway's parents very much."

Carla was on work related travel when Wanda passed away and was unable to attend her services. "I regret that," said Carla. "She was a classy and amazing woman."

CHAPTER 14
"I THINK I FOUND A CURE!"

In early 2020, Conway went to JB's Carpet Barn to look at new carpets for his home. He had been having a bad day; nothing was going right for him, but he had to complete this task. The salesperson helping him noticed Conway's damaged speech, and he point-blank asked him what was wrong. Conway told the man his story, the racing accident, the TBI, his NDE, the whole thing. The man introduced himself as Frank and told Conway he was a Christian. They started talking about that too. He told Conway that he didn't like going to Church; he chose to stay home and worship in his way. Their conversation continued for some time; they even debated specific issues regarding the Trinity, The Father, The Son, and The Holy Spirit. The two men traded phone numbers; Conway paid for his carpet and left.

Later that day, he received a text message from Frank at the carpet store, and then it all made sense to him. The message had a link to a site that explained a breakthrough procedure for stroke and TBI victims. The man's mother was a stroke victim and he had been checking into it, but decided against it. Once Frank understood Conway's speech problem he wanted to share the information with him. What Conway read excited him. Everything excited him with one exception: the cost of the new procedure.

Dr. Edward Tobinick, a Florida-based physician with practices in California, had created a new treatment for stroke and TBI victims in the form of a shot using the anti-inflammatory drug Etanercept.

Tobinick explains that the drug reduces neurological inflammation in an Institute for Neurological Recovery fact sheet published on his website. When the 25 –milligram shot is given in the back of the neck, the patient is placed at a 45-degree angle backward for five minutes, allowing the drug to enter the brain and spinal area through the cerebrospinal venous system, where it instantly fights inflammation. Four thousand people were treated with an 80 percent success rate during initial testing. Although most people were satisfied with a single dose, the doctor recommended a second shot if the patient improved.

Stoke and TBI victims were telling incredible stories of recovery from the treatment. The following are just two examples of the thousands that were reported:

An 88-year-old female stroke victim had been under constant care for three years before the treatment. With one shot, she was able to feed herself, she was able to walk better, and was able to think more quickly and clearly.

A 59-year-old male who had suffered a stroke 18 years prior had multiple issues. He could drive again with one treatment; his left leg was no longer dragging, and his head was clear.

Many were able to speak clearer and walk better, which attracted Conway to the treatment; however, there were several drawbacks to this treatment; one, the drug makers warn that continued use could lead to various serious side effects. Two, the "off label" use of the drug was not FDA approved; three, so most insurance carriers, including Medicare, would not cover the cost of the procedure; and finally, the cost of one treatment was **$4,800**. For Conway, that was entirely out of his budget. If you add transportation, hotel, meals, and medical costs, you are looking at nearly **$6,000 per visit.**

While discussing the procedure with his friend, Jason Lancaster, Jason asked Conway if he knew about a web-based program called Go Fund Me. Conway was unaware of the program, so Jason explained it to him. Conway liked the idea, and shortly after their discussion, a Go Fund page was set up. Conway wrote a short but informational explanation for the account, and Jason helped with the marketing. Racing websites, emails, texts, phone calls, and Facebook were contacted, and to Conway's surprise, the money started rolling in. By January 2022, there was $12,000 in the account, enough to pay for two treatments plus expenses; there were hundreds of people to thank.

In March, Conway scheduled an appointment and was off to Florida. His trip was filled with aggravating issues, one after another. First, his original flight was canceled because the pilot didn't show up. He got a last-minute flight with another airline, but halfway through the trip, they had to make an unplanned landing because of low fuel. By the time he got to Florida, the rental car company was closed. He caught a cab and got to the hotel at one that morning.

Conway went to the medical facility the following morning and underwent cognitive and physical testing. The results would be compared to the results of the same test after the treatment. He was strapped to a rotating bench, given the shot in the back of the neck, and turned head down. After about 15 minutes he was released from the bench he was released from the bench and given the same tests.

The doctor compared the tests; it showed his cognitive and walking movements had improved. Conway was still disappointed in his speech; there needed to be more improvement.

Once home, his friends and neighbors noticed the improvement in his gate, which made him feel better; however, his speech was the main issue, and he had already decided to get the second shot.

His next session was scheduled for July, and again Conway faced traveling challenges. First, the airline lost his bags and he almost lost his room due to various mix-ups when the hotel was inundated with immigrants who had been bused in on little notice. The staff at the hotel was overloaded and his room was never cleaned.

His second procedure was a carbon copy of the first with little if any, positive results. The drug worked better on stroke victims, and Conway knew it was a risk; there were no guarantees. But still, his trip home was depressing.

CHAPTER 15
SEARCHING FOR A WRITER

For twenty-two years, Conway searched for someone to put his story together in book form, not just a short story or a quickly forgotten news article, but a real story, explaining in detail what happened.

In his attempts to write, he fell short repeatedly in putting the pieces of his own experiences into words. Conway soon discovered that his TBI was at least a partial cause of his inability to put his thoughts down. There were also parts of the story he couldn't remember, for example, from the afternoon of October 3, 1993, to the morning of October 31, 1993, except for the NDE, he has no memory of that period. There were periods from October 31, 1993, to early January of 1994 that are also blank. He needed Carla and his friends to fill in those in.

It wasn't just partial memory loss that hampered his efforts. He found himself writing down the same story repeatedly. He had amassed several hundred pages of typed-out notes that were hard to piece together. In a rare moment for Conway, he realized he couldn't do it. He became frustrated and anxious with his inability to tell his own story.

How many authors had it been? In over twenty-two years, there were too many to count, the occasions where people would say, "I know someone," "I'll call you about it," "You need to meet with so and so," "Didn't they get back with you?" and the endless phone calls that went nowhere.

One day in 2015, he received a call, "Hello, I'm a published writer, and I understand you're looking for someone to write a book for you?" It was a female author who had been told about Conway's story and was interested. Due to his speech, he arranged a meeting and met her at home. Conway had to use his yellow pad and pen, and the writer reviewed his notes and written stories. "I'll get back to you soon," she said with a smile.

A few days later, she called Conway and declined to write his story. She had heard he was difficult to work with. "Difficult to work with? I haven't worked with anyone yet," Conway said with confusion.

A year later, Conway contacted another writer. The story was explained in a meeting, and Conway never heard from them again.

While at church one Sunday, a member approached Conway and gave him a name and phone number. "Text this man; he is interested in helping you tell your story." Conway contacted him. He was a Christian book author, and they met the following Sunday at Conway's church. The writer read what Conway had to say on his yellow pad, he looked over his massive collection of notes, "I'll do it, I'll write the story," he said. Pictures were taken of the two men together that day, and it looked like Conway was finally on his way.

A few days later, the man called and told Conway that there was one stipulation to his start date, "I'll need $20,000 upfront." Conway declined his offer and hung up the phone.

A few more years went by, and Conway was losing hope. The same old "I'll call you" or "get back to you" scenarios continued.

Conway was very active on Facebook, with over 1,000 people around the country on his friend list. In what he has admitted was "My last shot at getting a book done," he posted a request on his page one November day in 2022. "I'm requesting someone to step forward and help me write a book about my near-death experience." He went on to tell about his long journey and all the attempts to get it done. "I was very close to bagging the whole idea," said Conway. "I was thinking; it's been too long, no one cares because this story just isn't interesting." This time he got a response.

Author

I saw Conway's post and contacted him through Messenger. Over the next couple of weeks, we shared information about each other. During one conversation, we decided to give the book a try. I learned that Conway had difficulties with speech and that texting, Messenger, and email would be our best way to communicate.

I sent Conway an email with about 25 questions to start with. We started slowly because I wanted to connect the dots so to speak.

One day I received a large box in the mail with a three-ring binder in it, sent by Conway. It was stuffed full of typed stories and handwritten notes. His life in his own writing, the notes he had shared with numerous authors over the years.

There were dozens and dozens of pages going in numerous directions. I started piecing it together by the year and then by event. It was helpful, but it raised more questions than it answered. Our long communicative journey began.

I was several chapters into this book when one Saturday in late February of 2023, Conway and I were chatting on Facebook Messenger. Suddenly, with some confusion, I asked the following question:

Me- *"Do you remember how we met?"*

Conway- *"I was advertising on Facebook for an author."*

Me- *"No, that was in November of '22; we were already friends on Facebook."*

Conway- *"We were?"*

Me- *"Yes."*

Conway- *"When did we become friends on Facebook?'*

Me- *(After checking my friend's list) "It says August of 2021."*

Conway- *"Did I friend request you, or did you a friend request me."*

Me-?

Conway-?

When I first joined Facebook and learned the ins and outs, I promised to be conservative regarding my friend list. Some people will accept any request, but I wouldn't. At first, if I didn't know the person, I wouldn't accept a request. Then, after a few years, I would accept requests from people I wanted to get to know. I am very particular about who my friends are. My list has never been over 500 or so in the 15-plus years I've been on it. In addition, I won't send friend requests to people I don't know, period. It has to be a case of meeting you somewhere, through work, the car hobby, other interests, etc. Although Conway and I share the car hobby interest and drag racing, I have a fantastic memory, especially long-term. I had never heard of Conway, ever. And he had never heard of me.

It was a mystery at first; how did we become friends on FB? I know there is probably a logical explanation, but I can't find it. We became friends on Facebook in August of 2021? I couldn't remember seeing his name before November 2022, over a year since we had become friends. We had no mutual friends, not then, I checked.

After I looked this issue over for a few days, Conway did the same; it didn't take us long to figure it out, both laughing simultaneously. You already know the answer if you share some of the same beliefs as Conway and me. "How did we become friends?"

Divine intervention is an event that occurs when God becomes actively involved in changing some situation in human affairs.

CHAPTER 16
NEAR DEATH
EXPERIENCE ANALYZED

Conway knew in his heart that his near-death experience was real. In late 1993, about ten weeks after the accident, Conway started talking about it.

In 2000 he was encouraged to write a book about it, but life got in the way as well as all those doubters. It would be difficult to list the names of all the people that told Conway, "It was just a dream." He never once backed down; he knew it wasn't, it was real, and nothing on God's earth could convince him otherwise. In early 2023 Conway finally made contact with a person who fully understood his story and feelings. This is almost a story in itself.

According to experts like Dr. Raymond Moody, NDE, or near-death experiences, have been reported by thousands worldwide, with reports going back many centuries.

For this book, we interviewed Dr, Raymond Moody, considered by many as the "Grandfather" of near-death studies and research over the past fifty-eight years. Dr. Moody, or Ray, as he prefers to be called, has an impressive educational background. Born on June 30, 1944, he earned his Bachelor's degree in 1966, his Masters's degree in 1967, his first Ph.D. (philosophy) in 1969, a second Ph.D. (psychology) in 1972, and his MD degree in 1976. He has worked as a professor and forensic psychiatrist, published author, and was appointed chair in Consciousness Studies at UNR, University of Nevada at Reno.

As an undergraduate at the University of Virginia, Dr. Moody met Dr. George Ritchie, a psychiatrist, who told him about his experience at age twenty. He believed he journeyed to the afterlife after being dead for nine minutes.

He later wrote a book about the experience entitled "Return from Tomorrow." This prompted Dr. Moody to document similar accounts by others who had experienced clinical death. In 1975 he published the book "Life After Life" coining the phrase "near-death experience" or NDE.

In an interview with Jeffery Mishlove, Dr. Moody said the following:

"I don't mind saying that after talking with over a thousand people who have had these experiences and having experienced many times some of the baffling and unusual features of these experiences; it has given me great confidence that there is a life after death. I must confess to you, in all honesty, I have no doubt, based on what my patients have told me, that they did get a glimpse of the beyond."

Our interview with Dr. Moody was conducted on Wednesday, March 1, 2023. After introductions, which included the author and Conway Witten, Dr. Moody insisted we call him Ray, and we did. For the book, we will respect his experience and education and refer to him as Dr. Moody. He told us about his background, relationship with Dr. Richie, and several examples of his NDE research. We gave the Dr. a short history of Conway leading up to his NDE and read the experience authored by Conway some thirty years ago. Throughout all the years of NDE research and studies Dr, moody has come up with fifteen elements that best describe the NDE:

1. OBE, out-of-body experience
2. Peace and painlessness
3. Different perceptions of time and space
4. Other worlds
5. The Life Review
6. Light Phenomena or the Being of Light
7. Greeters or people of light
8. Experience in complete knowledge
9. The tunnel experience
10. Precognition
11. Rising rapidly into Heaven
12. Reluctance to return
13. Judgment Courts
14. Learning Environments
15. Heaven and, more rarely, hell

Dr. Moody told us that, on average, a person with an NDE would report between one to three elements on this list; sporadic cases have experienced all fifteen.

After review, we identified at least seven of the fifteen elements in Conway's NDE.

Out of body experience
Peace and painlessness
Different perceptions of time and space
Light phenomena or being of light
Reluctance to return
Judgment Courts
Heaven

We discussed Conway's experience in the hotel room in Topeka the night before the accident when he was overcome with grief and then became entirely peaceful. In addition, Conway asked Dr. Moody about some of the skeptics he has encountered over the past thirty years and their comments, mainly that he was in a dream state and/or drug-induced state. Dr. Moody explained it in the following way:

"Studies have shown that a higher percentage of people reporting their NDE were on no drugs. I don't think administering drugs for medical purposes induces an NDE; I think it will do the opposite. In regards to a dream or dream state, most dreams have a feeling of being unreal, where the NDE is beyond real."

Conway mentioned that most dreams are forgotten, the doctor agreed, and went on to say "Your experience will never be forgotten because it's vivid and everlasting."

Dr. Moody shared his thoughts on ancient Western philosophy, precisely Greek philosopher Plato, who wrote about one of the earliest near-death experiences. In his book "Republic," Plato recounts the story of a soldier who awoke after being dead for 12 days and shared his account of the journey to the afterlife. Plato also spoke on the pre-natal life of the soul and the soul's continued life after the body's death.

We contacted Dr. Bruce Greyson, now retired, and he directed us to an article he wrote on the subject of NDE through an email.

"We are particularly interested in studying NDEs that may bear on whether the mind can function outside the physical body and whether we may survive bodily death. One such type of experience is the so-called *veridical NDE*, in which experiencers acquire verifiable information they could not have obtained by any normal means. For example, some experiencers report seeing events at some distant location, such as another hospital room, or experiencers might meet a deceased loved one who then communicates verifiable information the experiencers had not known. Other NDEs that may bear on the mind/body

question include those in which mental functioning seems to be enhanced despite physiological evidence that the brain is impaired."

Dr. Greyson also directed us to New York Times bestselling author and international filmmaker Paul Perry, a lay expert on NDE issues who reviewed Conway's experience and agreed that it fit the description of an NDE.

We also spoke to David San Filippo, Ph.D. at National Louis University in Chicago, Illinois. Dr. San Filippo has been studying NDE for years and writes on the topic often. In his paper "The Value of the Awareness of the Near Death Experience," he writes, "Many experiencers report that towards the end of the experience they encounter a barrier; they are aware that if they go beyond the barrier, they will not be able to return to life."

In Conway's experience, he didn't want to leave the peaceful place he had found himself in and his discussion with the "Father." Also, in line with Dr. San Filippo's study regarding using the NDE to help reduce the fear of death among the elderly, Conway makes this statement early on after his NDE; "I no longer fear death because I know there is Heaven."

Oxford's definition of Heaven:

A place regarded in various religions as the abode of God (or the gods) and the angels and of the good after death, often traditionally depicted as being above the sky. "Those who practiced good deeds would receive the reward of a place in Heaven."

Over the years, Conway has heard all the skeptics regarding his reported NDE. In many circles, this is a controversial issue with plenty of critics. In Conway's case, one skeptical person questioned him on the basis of "Did you die?" The facts, in this case, show Conway was in respiratory arrest, but his heart never stopped.

In the book and later the movie "Heaven is Real," four-year-old Colton Burpo undergoes surgery twice due to his medical condition but is never clinically dead during the procedures, nor did he go into respiratory arrest; however, his account of an NDE is for the world to see. So, "near death" means precisely what it says.

In 1988, Dr. Pim van Lommel, a Dutch cardiologist, launched a prospective study of near-death experiences that spanned 10 Dutch hospitals. Three hundred forty-four survivors of cardiac arrest were included in the study. In 2001, his large-scale prospective study of near-death experiences after cardiac arrest was published in the medical journal "The Lancet." In 2007, his bestseller's first (Dutch) edition, "Consciousness Beyond Life: The Science of the Near-Death Experience," was published. "The NDE is an authentic experience that cannot be simply reduced to the imagination, fear of death, hallucination, psychosis, the use of drugs, or oxygen deficiency."

Lommel's landmark paper reveals several exciting things. First, NDEs have been shown to occur some minutes after the heart of a critical patient has stopped and at a time when "the brain ordinarily stops functioning and cortical activity becomes isoelectric." This implies that whatever the source or reason for these NDEs, it does not lay in ordinary, understood brain processes. Second, our recollection of NDEs is more like real than imagined memories.

As a research team from the University of Padova showed, "NDE memories and the real memories had the same amount of mnesic characteristics, and both were more complex and richer than imagined memories." That is to say, NDEs cannot be immediately dismissed as the fictional nonsense of near-death, at least regarding memory and recollection.

Finally, and perhaps most shockingly, people who have had an NDE can often recount things that happened while they were unconscious, such as an open-heart surgery.

Even more oddly, in a point considered by psychiatrist Dr. Bruce Greyson in a video for "Big Think," sometimes NDEs feature events that the experiencers couldn't have known about. In Greyson's case, a patient could "see" him talking to a colleague a corridor from where her bed lay, and he could think of no other explanation for how she knew that fact.

In some rarer cases, the NDE can be the last element on Dr. Moody's list, the experience of Hell.

Oxford's definition of Hell:

A place regarded in various religions as a spiritual realm of evil and suffering, often traditionally depicted as a place of perpetual fire beneath the earth where the wicked are punished after death. "Irreligious children were assumed to have passed straight to the eternal fires of Hell."

Recently, a Catholic Priest reported that his NDE resulted in a trip to Hell.

He claims to have seen men walking like dogs and demons torturing people with modern songs in a video he published on an internet site. He said, "I wouldn't wish it on my worst enemy."

The Priest says that immediately after his heart attack in February 2016, his spirit left his physical body and went down to Hell, entering through "the very center of the Earth." Though he says, "the things I saw there are indescribable," he did his best.

He saw a man with bulging eyes, and worse than that: He was wearing chains on his neck, and he was like a hellhound, and a demon was holding the chains.

Researchers, especially those from the International Association for Near-Death Studies, believe NDEs most likely happen due to a change in blood flow to the brain during sudden life-threatening events, like a heart attack, blunt trauma, or even shock. As your brain starts losing blood and oxygen, the electrical activity within the brain begins to power down.

During an NDE, your mind is left to keep working without its normal operational parameters. As hypothesized, the NDE leaves those who experience it with a real, sometimes traumatic memory, whether simply an oxygen shortage, some anesthesia, or a neurochemical response to trauma. We may not know how that memory happened, and unlike the Priest and his trip to Hell, victims may not want to recount it ever again, but it could change their life.

Near-death experiences come in a variety of stories, like the following one, told by the woman it happened to.

"I was involved in a serious car accident and had multiple injuries. Due to blood loss, I went into a coma. I remember seeing bright lights and feeling completely at peace. I was in an environment of love and saw and spoke to people I had known but had passed away.

During my conversations, a young man approached me and told me I had to go back. I told him I didn't want to; it was peaceful, and I was at peace. He once again said I had to go back, and I again refused. Finally, the young man approached me and said, "Mother, you have to go back." I laughed because I didn't have any children."

The woman woke up in a hospital room with several doctors and nurses by her side. The lead physician explained all of her injuries and gave her an estimated recovery time. He said, "And don't worry, the baby is fine; the injuries didn't affect it." The lady was puzzled, "What did you say?"

"Your baby is fine," the doctor repeated. The lady said, "What baby? The doctor said, "You're pregnant, didn't you know?"

Author

I believe Conway experienced an authentic NDE. During the many months I spent with him I quizzed him relentlessly on the subject, and from every angle, I approached him with question after question. He never backed down or changed his statement regarding additions or deletions. He wept and became angry at times, but he never changed his story.

During his many weeks of convalescence, he could not share what had happened to him. He knew he had experienced something rare and wonderful but couldn't describe it initially. His first opportunity was riding in the car with Carla when he saw the Christmas lights; he pointed to the sky and, in his slurred mumblings, said, "How did they get me down, Bright lights, how did they get me down?" His first opportunity to share the entire experience came in January of 1994, three months after it happened when he wrote the experience down on paper.

Conway would send me his comments about his experience from time to time that was not necessarily meant for the book, just talking about it from so many perspectives. I want to share them here.

"It was the calmest happiest place I ever experienced in my life."

"Why me, why did I get a glimpse of Heaven? Why did I survive?"

"I want this to be the cornerstone of my life."

"I didn't want to leave that place and for a long time, I didn't understand what had really happened."

There are numerous stories out there about NDE. Conway's is only one.

I want to share an experience I had. Although not an actual NDE, it has stayed with me for all these years.

In the early winter of 1959, when I was five years old, and in Kindergarten, I became sick. I was tired and listless; all I wanted to do was sleep.

I was taken to the local doctor, where tests were run with no results. I was taken to a specialist, and tests were run; this time, the doctor announced I probably had leukemia but more testing needed to be done. My parents were at wit's end, depressed, not knowing what was wrong. They asked their Presbyterian Minister to come to our home and pray for me, he did, and my parents were preparing themselves for my death. I was placed in the hospital when I became dehydrated, I couldn't stay awake long enough to eat or drink, and IVs were inserted. The Minister prayed for me almost every night in the hospital; I have memories of that and an experience; I won't call it an NDE, but I can recite what I experienced today, 64 years later.

I was walking in a cave-like dwelling, and large machines with lights blinking were on both sides of me; they resembled large computers of that era, reaching the top of the dwelling like giants.

As I continued walking, I saw a man in a white robe; his hands were pressed together as if in prayer; he looked at me and smiled; he said you would be well. I didn't see his lips move, but I could hear him talk. I can remember soon after that; I started to get better.

I was awake and terrified because of the activity around me. One day the doctor came in with good news; my mother was there. They were finally able to determine my problem, acute infectious mononucleosis. I can remember my mother crying right there, the doctor was hugging her, and I was given the largest glass of orange juice I had ever seen. I was so thirsty I drank it in seconds while the doctor told me to slow down.

I was released after two weeks in the hospital and four months of illness.

Was it a dream? Was it an NDE? I don't know. I shared this with Dr. Moody, and we discussed it; it's undetermined, but I can remember that event to this day; I can see it in my mind 64 years later.

What about the Bible? Are there any passages that talk about the NDE? In presenting the following, we must be cautious and tell the reader it is up to you to determine the meaning.

The apostle Paul wrote much of the New Testament. Is there evidence that Paul had an NDE that he describes in the Bible? If you look at **2 Corinthians, Chapter 12**, Paul is describing this remarkable experience when he says, "I went to the third heaven, and I had experiences that were so remarkable that I really can't describe them."

I know a man in Christ who, fourteen years ago, was caught up to the third Heaven. Whether it was in the body or out of the body, I do not know--God knows.

EPILOGUE

It took thirty years for Conway to find a new beginning. Finding a church he believed in renewed his faith in God, finding Dr, Moody confirmed his near death experience.

During that period, he nearly lost his life, and left his ability to speak clearly and walk normally on a drag strip in Topeka, Kansas.

The traumatic brain injury he suffered due to the racing accident also brought on other difficulties. Conway experienced depression brought on by post-traumatic stress, and experiencing personality changes he couldn't control. He no longer had the patience he once had; his temper was elevated, and he lost his confidence and his means to support himself. Ultimately Conway lost Carla, his home, and his father within just a few months. He contemplated suicide more than once, but throughout the ordeal, he never lost faith in God. That was his salvation; he beat the odds and survived the injury. Conway's faith in God is what helped him to rebuild his life. For him, to be where he is now is a miracle.

He also found someone to legitimize his near-death experience. Conway always knew it was real, a gift, an actual occurrence, something extraordinary. Now, the leading expert on the subject has confirmed it.

Conway identified what he thought were the actual causes of his crash. Most people say, "It was racing, man; stuff happens!" Conway disagrees. First, he was using rear wheels that were too narrow for the racing slicks. Goodyear recommended wider wheels for the size slicks he was using, but Conway knew that a narrower wheel would cause the tire to grow, giving him more speed at top end; however, it also caused less traction, a smaller surface patch. When Conway felt the car losing traction, he stayed in it and didn't let up on the throttle; he tried to drive out of it, it didn't work, and he lost control. You ask him why? He will tell you to this day, "I would do anything for speed, anything to win; that was my competitive nature."

It's early summer in Brandenburg, Kentucky, about 46 miles southwest of Louisville, and Conway is sitting in a lawn chair outside the racing engine shop of

Jason Lancaster. A cool breeze is blowing from the west, but it won't last long. The humid summertime air will soon be heavy, and the temps will climb into the high 80s. "Might as well enjoy the breeze while it lasts," says Conway to no one in particular.

The men working at the shop hang out on their lunch break, and the occasional joke is told while laughter fills the air.

Conway, who retired in 2018, spends a lot of time at the shop now. He occasionally troubleshoots, consulting with Jason and his crew on a project now and then; mostly, he likes the atmosphere, the milling machine, the running Dynamometer, and the sounds of engine building. Precise, technical work that brings back memories.

Conway, who will celebrate his 68th Birthday in the fall, has a simpler life now. He met his girlfriend, Debbie Jones, a few years ago. They enjoy each other's company, going to the movies, shopping, attending church, and sometimes watch TV together on weekend evenings.

He doesn't attend the drag races; no one close to him likes them, and he has lost interest. Hard to believe that a man with 33 national event wins, 27 national ET and MPH records, with hundreds of trophy wins at local tracks over twenty years would have lost interest. In retrospect, Conway isn't a spectator; he's a driver.

Conway was recently talking to the man that gave him the nickname "Assassin." Reno Zavagon, a pen name for Bret Kepner, the man who wrote the article about Conway's Super Stock Corvette, is a well-known automotive writer, drag racer, track owner, and national-level track announcer for many racing organizations.

After all these years, Conway was curious why he chose that name. Bret responded with the following answer:

"I think it was just based on the fact you were doing something nobody had ever done in that class. You were beating everyone, including all the known guys; it was a huge moment in super stock and drag racing history. I also needed to get the word "ass" in the article to associate it with the driver!"

Conway finished the build on his Shelby Daytona Coupe, it's a beautiful car, and he drives it in the warm months to car shows and events.

If you're looking for Conway and he's away from the shop, he might be at Gary Crain's house helping him with a MOPAR project. Gary and Conway have known each other since the early '70s when they played softball together. Gary was Conway's boss in a job he had early in life as well. Recently, Conway rebuilt the factory installed 426 Hemi engine out of Gary's 1966 Plymouth Satellite.

Conway's Church is Bethany Methodist in Louisville, and he attends every Sunday like clockwork. The Minister is Matthew Oaks, and he has been very supportive of Conway over the years.

Carla is retired too, married again for many years now. She loves to travel and spend time with her family. She goes to craft fairs occasionally and tries to keep things simple. "I choose to keep the good memories close and the bad ones at bay," she said softly.

Memories are special when you get older, and you can lose yourself in them and relive the better ones; try not to dwell on the bad ones; both tried to follow that example while the book was written, but it didn't always work.

As the author, I saw both Conway and Carla break down on several occasions, the emotion of the moment overwhelming them; it was understandable. They spent 18 years together; saw each other's success, Conway winning races on the track and Carla accomplishing her educational goals and receiving numerous promotions on the job. They shared their youth early in their marriage and faced the tragedy of Conway's accident, him nearly dying, and Carla showing her strength and compassion. Carla remained the pillar throughout Conway's recovery; he might not have made it through without her.

Although it was sad to write about their breakup, Conway and Carla eventually went on to lead happy lives; at times, both wondered what would have happened if they had stayed together; however, both of them understands those days are now gone.

Conway and Carla's friends throughout their relationship were Chuck Belanger, who is alive and well, living in the area; Gordon Holloway is well into his 80s now and still lives in Memphis; Mike Farrell is still racing; Tony Clark and his wife Donna are retired and so is Leon Clark, now almost completely blind but happy and adjusting to his condition. Bob Toy is retired and doing great these days, Mike Keown passed away several years ago, and Conway misses him dearly.

We contacted the CEO of the National Hot Rod Association, Mr. Peter Clifford. In our email, we explained the book project to him and asked if he or another NHRA representative would like to contribute in some way. Our goal was to phrase the NHRA Safety Safari Team for helping to save Conway's life that day in Topeka and to get a statement about their safety history.

Mr. Clifford declined, as did several other division managers and the current director of their track safety efforts. Our only intention was to give credit to their organization, which we did anyway.

To show you how fate works in our lives, we must take you back to that tragic day in Topeka, October 3, 1993, and the NHRA Sears Craftsman Nationals. Conway's racing opponent in the finals and the final race of Conway's career was Jeff Krug, who went on to win the race and the Wally.

Jeff lived in the Los Angeles area but was born in Canada, moving to the States as a child with his family. He worked his way up in a construction corporation from a laborer to a managing director and V.P. Jeff was a solid racing competitor and a great guy.

A local Topeka newspaper interviewed Jeff after the race with Conway on that October day in 1993. He had this to say:

"Once I shut down and got stopped, I saw the ambulance and emergency crews rolling, I knew it was bad. I said a prayer for Conway. This was the most depressing win I have ever experienced."

Jeff and crew members went to the hospital the following day but were not allowed to see Conway. Carla was there, and Jeff greeted her, giving her a hug and thoughtful comments about recovery.

Three and a half years later, on April 20, 1997, during his first NHRA event of the year at Famoso Drag Strip in Bakersfield, California, Jeff crashed during a race; tragically, he died at the scene. He was only 40 years old.

Once again, we take you back to October 3, 1993, at the NHRA Sears Craftsman Nationals in Topeka; Conway dispatched competitor and well know businessman John Lingenfelter during an early round in the Competition Eliminator Class.

John was a well-known racer in several classes and the founder of Lingenfelter Performance Engineering; he was a brilliant innovator and well-liked by all.

Nine years after Conway dispatched competitor and well known businessman John Lingenfelter during an early round in Competition Eliminator Class, on October 27, 2002, during an NHRA Summit Sports Compact drag racing event in Pomona, California, John was critically injured in a crash. First Responders administered CPR and revived him at the scene; he was rushed to a local hospital, where reports indicated he had suffered a broken neck and was paralyzed from the neck down. One month later, while in surgery, John lapsed into a coma and remained in that state until his death on Christmas day, 2003. He was 58 years old.

In 2006, Conway and his friend Gary Crain traveled to the US Nationals in Indianapolis. It was early on Monday, September 4, Labor Day. As Conway and Gary went to get breakfast at a cafeteria by the weigh scales, he saw several members of the NHRA Safety Safari Crew standing around talking. Carefully, Conway checked out their names embroidered on their uniform shirts. Sure enough, there was Dan Brickey, the lead NHRA EMT who saved his life that day in Topeka. They had never formally met. Dan had come to the hospital in Topeka and introduced himself to Carla. He told her everything about the rescue. Conway was in a coma then, and months later, Carla told him the story of her meeting Dan. He'd always remembered that name.

Conway walked up and said, "Hello!" In his damaged speech, Dan didn't understand him, nor did he recognize him; it had been nearly 15 years since the crash. Always carrying his yellow legal pad and pen, Conway wrote down his information.

"I'm Conway Witten; you saved my life at Topeka in '93. Do you remember me now?"

Dan looked stunned at first, then he grabbed Conway, and they embraced, tears in both men's eyes; it was a special moment for both.

They chatted for a while, Dan asking numerous questions and Conway relying on his legal pad. The men embraced again and said their goodbyes; it was time for Dan to go to work. Two years later, Dan would die, just days after the 2008 US Nationals. When Conway heard of his death, he paused, overcome with emotion. "This man had my life in his hands," said Conway, trembling at the thought of the crash. "Life is so fragile; he certainly knew his job."

Bob Unkefer, who grew up in Liberty, Mo, while attending NHRA events at Kansas City International Raceway, where he first started racing and announcing, was the track announcer at Topeka when Conway crashed.

"To this day, I can watch that run in my mind, my first NHRA National event as an announcer," Bob said, "I knew it was horrific as it unfolded right in front of me. I had never announced a crash at the track before and was somewhat intimidated by the event." Bob deferred to Dave Mac and Bob Frey for their guidance, two other NHRA Veteran announcers in the tower that day. Bob Frey walked Bob Unkefer through the proper procedures, and he got the job done.

"I remember there was a lot of silence in the tower while rescuers attended Conway; we could hear the radio chatter and knew things weren't good. A lot of prayers were answered that day!" said Bob.

Bob became Facebook friends with Conway, and on the twentieth anniversary of the crash, he shared the above comments in a post. Sadly, Bob passed away in April of 2022; he was 68 years old.

From the summer of 1973 to the fall of 1993 Conway owned and raced nine different cars. He went through the list one day to determine their current fate to the best of his memory.

The 1965 Mustang convertible was sold to a local man in the Louisville area and used as a daily driver for several years. Actual location now is unknown.

The first 1964 Mustang hardtop was sold to a junkyard; the body was completely rusted out.

The six cylinder dragster was sold and raced for several more years; its current whereabouts is unknown.

The second 1964 Mustang hardtop was sold and continues to race today.

At his home with the author, Conway points to an article about his racing and near death experience, written a long time ago and published on a now retired website. At times, he still carries his yellow legal pad and pen, writing on it so someone not used to him can understand. He points to his statement, "Read this," he writes.

> *"I believe I'm like Jacob in the Bible; when he encountered God, his hip was dislocated. God did it so Jacob would never forget. You cannot have an encounter with God and not be scathed. My speech is like Jacob's hip. The fact that I can't speak is so I'll never forget.*

Conway pondered a recent comment by a church member. The statement was made after learning about Conway's experience for the first time. "You saw God," said the church member. Writing on his yellow pad, Conway politely corrected the member, "You don't see God; there are no words to describe it. It is more like I experienced God, but that doesn't come close to telling you about what I experienced. Your past, present, and future don't matter anymore because you are in a different dimension.

I can remember being impressed by the clarity and calmness of this place. All without the pressure of time always haunting you, it was very liberating. Satan causes confusion, which is why Heaven is so good. For once, there is no confusion; everything is crystal clear, no pain, no regrets, no guilt, no envy, none of the things that are constantly on our minds. It's a Satan-free zone!"

Want to know more?

International Association for Near Death Studies

Provides first-hand near-death experience accounts offering insights and perspectives about consciousness and what happens after we die. The International Association for Near Death Studies is a membership organization that promotes research, education, and support around near-death and related experiences.

Brain Research Foundation

As the nation's oldest brain research organization, we've seen the impact that undesignated giving can have. Our grants fund a broad scope of projects that help scientists explore a wide range of neurological disorders.

National Hot Rod Association

The National Hot Rod Association is a governing body which sets rules in drag racing and hosts events all over the United States and Canada. With over 40,000 drivers in its rosters, the NHRA claims to be the largest motorsports sanctioning body in the world.

GLOSSARY

1320: Number of feet in a 1/4 mile.

Air Foil: also known as a wing - a stabilizer used to create down force, which increases stability and tire traction at high speeds.

Bench Racing: The act of telling racing stories to your friends and family

Burnout: Spinning the rear tires in water (see Water Box) at a high RPM to heat them, clean them, and leave a rubber patch on the tack for better traction. Produces billows of white smoke.

Burned Piston: When a cylinder runs lean (too much air in the air-to-fuel mixture) and excessive heat burns or melts, or incinerates the piston within the combustion chamber due to a lack of fuel within its cylinder.

Christmas Tree: or the Tree, as it is often called, is the electronic starting line device between lanes on the starting line, utilizing a sequential "countdown" of lights calibrated to within .0001 of a second accuracy. See Tree.

Chute: Short for parachute, used for high-speed braking.

Door slammer: A drag car with doors (as opposed to a dragster).

Drag Race: An acceleration contest from a standing start between 2 vehicles over a measured distance (usually 1/8 or 1/4 of a mile). Bracket Drag Racing is based on an E.T. handicap. In Bracket Racing, the slower vehicle receives a head start.

Elapsed Time: Also known as E.T. - Time required for a vehicle to travel from the starting line to the finish line. The time is usually measured to 1/1000 of a second. A car "starts" or triggers the E.T. timer by tripping the staging beam and ending when the vehicle breaks a similar light beam at the finish line to complete the timing.

Eliminations: After qualifying, vehicles race two at a time, resulting in one winner from each pair. Winners continue in tournament-style competition until one remains.

E.T.: See Elapsed Time.

Green Light: Light on the tree to signal the driver to go.

Groove: A path of rubber laid down by other cars on the track surface.

Handicap: The difference, in time, of 2 vehicles in a Bracket Race. The slower vehicle receives a head start based on the difference between horsepower to weight factor.

Headers: Fine-tuned exhaust system that routes exhaust from the engine. Replaces conventional exhaust manifolds.

Hole Shot: Having a quicker reaction time than your opponent, gained by faster reflexes at the start of a race.

Lights: It has two different meanings. It can refer to the starting lights on the Christmas Tree or the top-end lights' or 'eyes,' which talk about the photocells near and at the finish line (i.e., the last 66 feet).

Loose: When a car loses traction or gets out of the groove.

MOPAR Fans: Nick name for Chrysler, Dodge, and Plymouth fans.

NHRA: National Hot Rod Association

NOS: Nitrous Oxide is typically used during races because it has the potential to provide a short burst of power to a vehicle. The compound does this by increasing the amount of oxygen present in the engine's cylinders during combustion. (It is used both legally and illegally in drag racing. In the era Conway was racing it would have been illegal to use it.)

On The Trailer: Term used for drivers eliminated from the competition.

Rail: Dragster

Reaction Time: The electronically clocked time it takes a driver to react to the green starting light on the tree, measured in thousandths of a second.

Red Light: A red light occurs if a car starts before the green light comes on. During the competition, this will immediately give the win to the opponent.

RPM: Engine speed is defined by the revolutions per minute of the engine crankshaft.

Shutdown Area: Distance between the finish line and the sand trap where cars slow down after the race.

Slick: Race tires without tread.

Staged: A driver is staged when the car's front wheels are right on the starting line, and the yellow light below the pre-staged light is glowing.

Tech: Inspections who are the magistrates of drag racing. They verify the legality and safety of every vehicle in competition through lengthy examinations known simply as tech.

Time Slip: the results of the race. A piece of paper listing the reaction time, 60' time, 330' time, 1/8 mile time and speed, 1000' time, and 1/4 mile time and speed.

Top End: Far side of the track near the finish line.

Traction Zone: The area on the track surface near the starting line where fresh rubber is, allowing better traction on the start.

Treed: Having significantly worse reaction time than the opponent.

Wally: NHRA trophy named after NHRA founder Wally Parks.

Water Box: The designated area for pre-race burnouts, named for the water trough, in which the tire heating exercise is performed.

Wheelie Bars: Devices placed at the vehicle's rear to prevent excessive front wheel lift.

ABOUT THE AUTHOR

Mark Brothers was born in 1954 and grew up in southeastern Illinois. He started his award-winning career in safety management while in mining and became a published freelance writer in the late 1970s. While in safety, as a supervisor and manager, Mark worked underground coal and surface and underground gold. He was general manager of a safety consulting and training facility, a division safety manager for an internationally based engineering and construction company, traveling the world as the resident expert in behavioral-based safety programs, and corporate director of safety and risk management for a multi-state construction corporation. He retired in 2016 and started writing books, primarily auto-related subjects. He has three children and six grandchildren and lives in Northeastern Utah on a small ranch with his wife. They have Boston Terriers, cats, and horses, and they grow and harvest hay from their pasture and care for a large garden every year. Mark's hobbies are collecting and showing classic and muscle Fords, collecting Ford memorabilia, and writing. In addition, Mark and his wife, Garna, volunteer their time to transport rescue animals to new homes throughout the year.

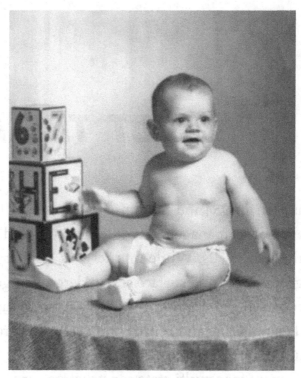

Conway at six months
Witten Family Collection Photo

Conway at 17
Witten Family Collection Photo

Harden and Barbara Pace – Circa 1950s
Pace Family Collection Photo

Carla at six months
Pace Family Collection Photo

Carla at six years old
Pace Family Collection Photo

Carla at 15
Pace Family Collection Photo

Carla and Conway Wedding -1981
Pace Family Collection Photo

Family -1981
Pace Family Collection Photo

Carla
Witten Family Collection Photo

Conway
Witten Family Collection Photo

Conway and Carla
Witten Family Collection Photo

The last Mustang Conway raced. A 1964 Hardtop
Witten Family Collection Photo

Chuck Belanger on left, Conway on right. First National
NHRA Class Championship with Corvette-1982
Eric Brooks Photo

Portion of Super Stock Magazine article about Conway's Corvette
Super Stock Magazine Photo

Conway's Super Stock Olds in action
Auto Imagery Photo

Conway wins class championship at US Nationals – 1987
Eric Brooks Photo

Conway behind the wheel of the DeFrank Camaro
Witten Family Collection Photo

Conway winning class at Pomona in the DeFrank Camaro
Auto Imagery Photo

Conway (center) winning another 'Wally' with crew members
Mike Keown (left) and Kenny Morris(right)
Witten Family Collection Photo

Conway posing with his second dragster, the car he crashed in at Topeka.
Witten Family Collection Photo

A portion of Conway's trophies.
Witten Family Collection Photo

One of many class and world record certificates Conway received over the years.
Witten Family Collection Photo

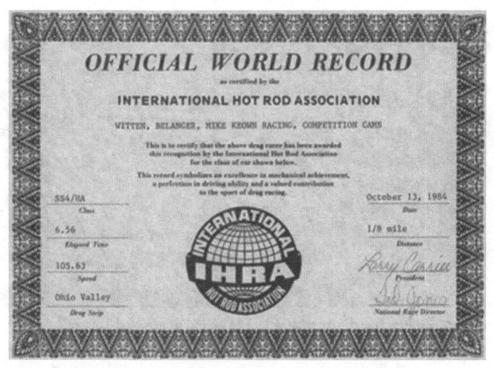

One of many class and world record certificates Conway received over the years.
Witten family Collection Photo

Conway and his crew winning 'Best Engineered Car' from the NHRA.
Auto Imagery Photo

Conway lines up for what would be his last drag race at Topeka.
Witten Family Collection Photo

Conway's crash at Topeka.
Witten Family Collection Photo

Conway's crash at Topeka.
Witten Family Collection Photo

Conway's crash at Topeka.
Witten Family Collection Photo

The Life Flight Helicopter taking Conway to the hospital.
Witten Family Collection Photo

Conway learning to walk again during rehab.
Witten Family Collection Photo

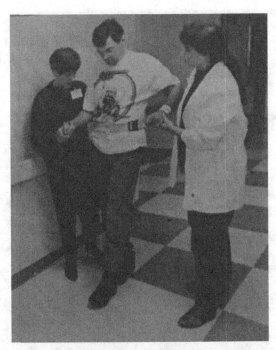

Conway learning to walk again during rehab.
Witten Family Collection Photo

Conway with NASCAR great Bobby Allison
Witten Family Collection Photo

Conway and Carla a few years after the crash
Pace Family Collection Photo

Conway built this Shelby Daytona Kit Car by hand.
Witten Family Collection Photo

Conway writing on his famous 'yellow pad' in order to communicate.
Witten Family Collection Photo

Conway with his Kentucky Motors Sports induction plaque.
Witten Family Collection Photo

Conway today.
Witten Family Collection Photo

Carla today.
Pace Family Collection Photo

The 'Puckett – Witten' Mustang
Witten Family Collection Photo

Conway in the Corvette.
Auto Imagery Photo

Conway doing burnout in the Olds.
Witten Family Collection Photo

Conway in action in the DeFrank Camaro.
Witten Family Collection Photo

Several drivers displayed this sign on their race cars while Conway recovered from the crash.
Bobby Davis Family Collection Photo

Conway wearing the 'Trust Me' T-shirt.
Witten Family Collection Photo

Conway on TV.
Witten Family Collection Photo

Conway heats up the rear tires of the DeFrank Camaro.
NHRA Rules Book Photo- Photographer unknown

Conway's last Mustang with new owner still racing.
Witten Family Collection Photo

Conway's Corvette with new owner still racing.
Witten Family Collection Photo

Conway lifts the wheels on the Super Stock Olds.
Kenneth Allen Photo

Author Mark Brothers poses with his 1963 427 Galaxie
Brothers Family Collection Photo

Conway pulling the chutes in the dragster.
Auto Imagery Photo

Conway Racing at Edgewater Drag Strip.
Auto Imagery Photo

Bill and Wanda Witten-Circa 1950s.
Witten Family Collection

Conway Racing at National Trail Raceway.
Auto Imagery Photo
Back Cover – Conway in the Corvette, the DeFrank Camaro, and the dragster.
Auto Imagery Photos